Scenes from
an ABSOLUTELY FABULOUS 2 life. . . .

EDINA . . .

On having had her daughter Saffron by Caesarean: Yes, I
know I had a Caesarean, darling. But how do you
think it feels for Mummy to wake up every morning
and look down and see her stomach smiling back up
at her?

On being arrested for stealing champagne: Have you any
idea how much champagne costs these days? I was
forced to steal it. My daughter wouldn't have allowed
me to buy it.

On paying taxes: Why not just have a "Stupidity Tax," just
tax the stupid people?

On her daughter: Excuse me if I die prematurely of passive
boredom, or dull-as-dishwater-daughter-induced stress.

PATSY . . .

On an old acquaintance: She was so anally retentive she
couldn't sit down for fear of sucking up the furniture.

On checking out her hospital room: No bloody mini-bar.

On today's retro music scene: These bands are just second-rate
crap bands that I didn't like the first time around.

On reasons to go to Marrakech: Easygoing sex with gorgeous underage youths. . . .

ABSOLUTELY 2

jennifer saunders

FABULOUS

POCKET BOOKS
New York   London   Toronto   Sydney   Tokyo   Singapore

This book is a work of fiction. Names, characters, places and incidents are products of the author's imagination or are used fictitiously. Any resemblance to actual events or locales or persons, living or dead, is entirely coincidental.

POCKET BOOKS, a division of Simon & Schuster Inc.
1230 Avenue of the Americas, New York, NY 10020

Copyright © 1994 by Mr. & Mrs. Monsoon Ltd 1996

Published by arrangement with BBC Worldwide Ltd.

ISBN: 0-671-00021-7

First Pocket Books trade paperback printing September 1996

10 9 8 7 6 5 4 3 2 1

POCKET and colophon are registered trademarks of Simon & Schuster Inc.

Cover design by Steven Ferlauto
Cover photo courtesy of BBC Worldwide Ltd.

Printed in the U.S.A.

Photographs © BBC

Contents

hospital 1

death 27

morocco 53

new best friends 81

poor 105

birth 129

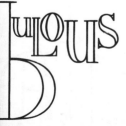

Characters

EDINA In her very late thirties. Two children both by different husbands. Son at university. Daughter at school. Lives life at a manic pace. Is neurotic, successful, in charge of her own company which is a Public Relations/Design/Fashion business. She is obsessed with keeping up with the times.

SAFFRON Edina's teenage daughter. She is the complete opposite of her mother. Living with her mother forces her to take on the mothering role.

PATSY In her forties. Edina's best friend. Magazine editor, but spends most of her time hanging around drinking and smoking fags and joints, and trying to get everybody else to do likewise.

BUBBLE Edina's secretary. In her twenties. There is no obvious reason for her employment except she has the right looks and is good at booking lunches.

Cast List

Edina · JENNIFER SAUNDERS
Patsy · JOANNA LUMLEY
Saffron · JULIA SAWALHA
Mother · JUNE WHITFIELD
Magda · KATHY BURKE
Catriona · HELEN LEDERER
Fleur · HARRIET THORPE
Antonia · JENNIFER PIERCEY
Sarah · NAOKO MORI
Nurse · LLEWELLA GIDEON
Nurse Mary · ORLA BRADY
Mr Simpson · DAVID HENRY

Guest Stars

'Patsy' · MANDY RICE-DAVIES
'Saffy' · HELENA BONHAM-CARTER
'Justin' · RICHARD E. GRANT
'Nurse' · SUZI QUATRO
'Mother' · GERMAINE GREER
Voice of Lady Penelope · SYLVIA ANDERSON

scene one Edina's kitchen. Day one.

Saffron is surrounded by files, notes and university things but is reading a newspaper feature. Edina is flicking through a pile of newspapers.

Saffron Tut–tut–tut–tut–tut . . .

Edina (*To Saffy.*) Tut–tut–tut–tut–tut–tut–tut . . . Don't get all tutty, darling. When Patsy comes here I want you to treat her with a little bit of respect, all right?

Patsy enters, removing a blanket from over her head. She is frenetic.

Patsy Click, click, click, flash, flash, flash, click, click flash, flash, flash, Guys, Guys, Guys – just give me a break, darling, just give me a break, sweetie. I have a life to lead . . . this way, Patsy. Click, click. (*Goes to window.*) Fellas, fellas, sweeties, darlings, can you just leave me alone? Click, click, click, flash, flash, flash. Click click click . . . Patsy, Patsy, Patsy . . . ooh, huh! (*She sits.*)

Edina Are you all right, darling? You're not letting this get to you, are you?

Patsy No, of course not.

Edina Little bit of Bolly?

Patsy Yeah, just a smidge. Oh, are these today's?

Edina Yes, sweetie.

Patsy Anything in them?

Edina Not much, darling, no.

Saffron picks one up and reads.

Saffron 'MP in drug-crazed sex romp shock with fash-mag slag'.

Patsy Damn.

Edina I know. Well there is that . . . Thank you very much, sweetie. (*To Patsy.*) Well, in fact, you're front page in most of them, darling, but it has only been a day, you know.

Patsy Oh . . . I mean who could still possibly be interested in reading all this?

ABSOLUTELY fab

Saffron His wife?

Patsy (*Hissing at her.*) Listen, Saffy. I am the victim in this case. I mean he's just using me for publicity. He's just riding on my back to get his pathetic little face in the papers.

Edina Exactly, sweetie. Patsy has had the hassle and trauma. She's been forced to leave her flat, darling.

Saffron Forced? Even the cockroaches left that hole of their own accord.

Edina Darling, they are trying to make out, darling, that Patsy is some kind of sex-crazed, morally-corrupt, drunken, high-class prostitute, darling.

Saffron Pretty accurate so far.

Edina and Patsy react. Edina reads the headlines.

Edina Look at this. 'Four-letter Patsy in MP sex row' . . .

Patsy 'Orgy of alcohol and sex near MP's home' . . .

Edina That's ridiculous. Those bastard scum filth of the Press, darling . . .

Saffron Well, make up your mind! One minute they're scum and the next you're giving them lunch and pouring booze down their throats in the great name of PR.

Edina Booze? Booze? Sweetie? Booze, darling? Is that what they call it down the Uni bar? Booze, sweetie, is it? Will you be popping in there, darling, after a hard day's lecture for some half-a-pint of shandy booze? Some pork scracklings? Oh, God, where was I? (*Returns to reading the newspapers.*) Oh . . . 'Illicit passion for MP's posh-clothes mag-gal pal' . . . 'Shocked wife of MP keeps silent'.

Patsy/Edina Bitch!

Patsy Bitch!

Edina 'Queen furious' . . . Oh, that's not you.

Patsy (*Picks up another newspaper.*) Oh, well, heigh-ho, Eddy. (*Pours*

2 | 3

more champagne.) I mean, you know, let them write what they want ... (*Starts to read another feature.*) Continued on page 5. I mean I shall just rise above it. I shan't let this thing affect me in ... (*Notices something in particular.*) Bastard! No! No! No!

Edina Who, who? Where, where? What, quick what? What, what? Show, show, show ... (*Patsy hands her the newspaper. Edina reads aloud.*) 'Source is ...'

Patsy No, no, no – further ...

Edina 'Patsy is ...' Uh?

Patsy Yes?

Edina Aged forty-seven!

Patsy Aagh! I'll sue!

Saffron (*To Edina.*) Well, how old is she?

Edina shrugs.

Patsy I'm thirty-nine.

Saffron And I'm an ovum.

Patsy tears up the paper and throws it in the bin.

Patsy Oh ... it's just not fair.

Mother enters reading newspaper headlines.

Mother Another pig-ugly MP making a fool of himself with some scrawny old hooker, I see.

Patsy (*Grabs the paper from Mother, looks at the photo and shreds the newspaper in the food blender.*) Old? Old! Old, Old, Old!

Mother Nothing like a good old sex scandal. Bit more exciting than the ones in my day.

Edina God, what was it in your day? 'Woman shows ankle to chimney-sweep shock'!

Patsy You know, in my day ...

Saffron Your day. Which century was that?

Patsy . . . in my day there was a sense of style about the whole thing. You know, Christine Keeler and Mandy Rice-Davies . . . little gorgeous little women who kept their mouths shut and just looked gorgeous, and gave the whole thing an air of dignity. You know, that's the way I shall play it, Eddy, not like these two-a-penny tarts of recent times, you know, kiss-and-tell, blurt it all out for the promise of a quick buck and instant fame. Not me, sweetie, my lips are sealed. (*Mimics zipping up her lips.*)

Edina You'll do *Hello!* magazine though?

Patsy (*Promptly unzips her lips.*) Oooh, yeah.

Edina Yeah, you might as well do it in the comfort of your own home, sweetie.

scene two Interior Edina's hallway. Day two.

Patsy is looking in the hall mirror putting on her facelifts. She is overdressed. The doorbell goes.

Patsy Oh, Eddy! Eddy! The people from *Hello!* are here. (*Opens the front door.*) Hello.

Antonia That's right. Antonia. (*She enters looking around the hall.*) Oh, it's interesting . . . rustic, ethnic.

Patsy Would you like to follow me into my gracious drawing-room?

scene three Interior Edina's kitchen. Day two.

Saffron is sitting with her friend Sarah. They have a pile of books and folders on the table. Edina is rifling through a couple of large packing boxes, unwrapping lamps, ashtrays and ethnic ornaments, swearing rather a lot.

Edina Sweetie, darling, could you just stop that a minute and just come and help me here?

Saffron gets up to help Edina unwrap ornaments from brown paper.

Edina I'm trying to unwrap all these things. They're all *objets* from my shop, darling, so keep the price-tags showing. The woman from

Hello! magazine is here and I haven't finished decorating the room.

Saffron Why bother?

Edina Because, sweetie, what you can't tell about a person by what they have chosen to be seen on their coffee table, isn't worth knicker-elastic. What do you think, darling? Look, look, look. What do you think? It's an eskimo papoose.

She produces a scruffy old papoose. Saffron turns her nose up at it.

Edina Don't look like that, sweetie. Any chance of a quick buck in the Arctic and they'd tip the babies out and ship 'em down, I can tell you.

Sarah (*To Saffron.*) You know, I think it's going to be really great if you move into the university's halls. I'm really really enjoying it. I mean, it takes a while to get used to it, you know all the noise and everything, like other people coming and going all the time, and other people's sound systems.

Saffron Sounds like home.

Sarah But you've got to get used to it if you're moving in.

Edina is about to exit but hearing what Sarah says stands still in shock. Then exits.

Saffron Oh . . . would you like another Aqua Libra?

Sarah Um . . . I don't suppose you've got any low-alcohol cider, have you? Cos that's what everyone's drinking at the moment!

Saffron Well, no actually. I don't drink.

Sarah Oh! You should give it a try. It's brilliant. You know last night, at a party, I drank a whole can!

scene four Interior Edina's sitting-room. Day two.

Patsy is draped on the sofa. Antonia is looking out of the window. Patsy is pert and Antonia is shuffling around making a note of the furnishing, muttering 'Conran', 'Osborne and Little', etc.

ABSOLUTELY fa

Antonia Now, where am I?

Patsy Sorry?

Antonia Where am I here?

Patsy In my gracious drawing-room.

Antonia No, I mean where is this?

Patsy looks confused.

Antonia Shepherd's Bush?

Edina (*Runs in laden with her 'objets', and stubs her toe on the door frame.*) Ow, ow, ow. Holland Park. *Holland Park* . . . not the outskirts, either. It's not the edge of Holland Park. This is the rich heartland of Holland Park, here, all right? Is the photographer here yet?

Antonia No, we never do photos on the same day. Next week.

Edina Oh God. (*Peering over Antonia's shoulder and looking at her notebook.*) It has a seventy-foot living-room, west-facing garden, £1.5 million.

She exits. Antonia sits down and looks at Patsy, studying her face hard. She really hasn't a clue who she is.

Antonia Right, let's, er, kick off, shall we? (*She selects a piece of paper and puts the rest away.*) Is it important to have lovely things around you?

Patsy/Antonia Yes . . .

Patsy resenting the interruption.

Antonia Is it a miracle that you're walking again?

Patsy It is a miracle that I can walk at all. I bless the wonder of life and the newness of living.

scene five Interior Edina's kitchen. Day two.

Edina is clutching her bad toe. Saffron and Sarah are at the table.

Sarah Jed might be around tomorrow night as . . . um . . . he and I sort of hang out a bit. You know . . . catching up on lecture notes and that sort of thing.

Saffron Ooooooh!

They laugh.

Sarah No, nothing like that . . . I know what you're thinking.

Edina crosses to the sink, turns on the tap and tries to bathe her toe under the running water.

Edina You may be sorely disappointed there . . .

Sarah Although the other night he did get locked up in our part of the halls . . .

Edina Poor bastard.

Sarah . . . And he did have to sleep on the floor of my room but . . .

Edina Only because he couldn't chew through the restraints with his bare teeth I should imagine.

Sarah You see, Jed's really, really lovely but he's . . .

Edina (*To Saffron.*) Oh, listen, could you just shut Titty Caca here up for a second. (*She is trying to soothe her bad toe by bathing it in a small glass pot.*) You know I'm just feeling . . . (*Dips toe in pot.*) Aaaargh! Oh, that's better. (*To Saffy.*) Now, listen you, I said you could go to university, darling, I did not say you could move into the residential home.

Saffron I'm only thinking of moving into the Halls of Residence because it is easier for me, all right?

Edina Oh, easier for you. Easier for you. I can see the headline now, can't you, sweetie? 'Home Alone Mother left to fend for herself while good-time daughter shacks up student-style.' 'I left her with a neighbour and friend,' she says. Oh, yes. Oh, yes. (*She has got her toe stuck in the glass pot.*) Oh bugger. Oh! Oh, God, help Mamma, sweetie. Help Mamma, darling. (*Then as Saffy pulls the pot off.*) Aaaah!

scene six Interior Edina's sitting-room. Day two.

Antonia is now mid-interview. Patsy is struggling.

Antonia And when will the baby be born? Do you hope to have a big family? (*Pauses, realizing she has come with the wrong questions.*) Oh, of course, how stupid of me. Those questions were transparently written for a much younger woman!

Patsy glares at her. Antonia sorts through her notes.

Antonia And you're not Annabel Croft?

Patsy (*Thoroughly put-out.*) No, I'm Patsy Stone.

Antonia Stone? Oh! Did your life change much after *Basic Instinct*?

scene seven Interior Edina's kitchen. Day two.

Edina is sitting at the table examining her toe. Saffy and Sarah are working. Edina slings her foot up on the table and reaches for the telephone.

Edina (*On the telephone.*) Yeah? Bonjour . . . oui . . . (*Ad-libs some foreign phrases.*) Das rectum . . . Oh, God . . . four bloody languages and they can't even specialize in one. Just put me through to Zermatt, Zermatt . . .

Saffron Who are you calling?

Edina My doctor. Philip, darling. He's skiing in Switzerland. (*Speaking into the telephone.*) Hallo? . . . Hallo? . . . Philip? . . . Philip . . . Yes, it's Edina . . . Um, you know this foot of mine, darling? Yeah, I just bashed it on the door frame. It's very painful . . . Huh? . . . Huh? . . . (*To Saffron.*) Oh, God, he's just hit the grand slalom. I can't hear him for the wind noise now.

Patsy (*Entering.*) Eddy . . .

Edina Oh, Pats, darling. How did it go?

Patsy Do these work? (*Referring to her DIY facelift.*)

BULLOUS

Edina For how old, sweetie?

Patsy Oh . . . thirty-five?

Edina You might need a few more for thirty-five I think, darling.

Patsy Well, how much more?

Saffron A bungy-jump with the elastic tied to the back of your head should get that back into shape.

Edina (*On the phone.*) Yes? Ssh . . . (*Skiing with him*) . . . Yes? Shh . . . Yes? Shh . . . operation . . . (*To Saffy.*) Darling? (*To phone.*) . . . hospital? . . . Yes, all right . . . all right . . . thank you. (*Hangs up. Nodding solemnly.*) Did you catch that, darling? I've got to go into hospital.

Patsy Hospital, Eddy? I'm coming with you.

Edina Oh, God, I'll have to pack and order the ambulance and everything.

Saffron Why don't you take your car?

Edina Because, sweetie, I do not pay huge insurance premiums so I can just drive myself to hospital. All right? And not stay over night, okay? Come on, Pats, which one shall we go to? The Cromwell? The Heritage?

Patsy Champneys?

Edina Ooohh – yeah – they've got a pool. Have they got a pool?

They exit.

scene eight Exterior Edina's house. Day three.

Edina and Patsy are both in wheelchairs about to go into the ambulance. Neither of them looks unwell, but both are trying to appear that way. They are lapping up attention from curious neighbours. Edina is wheeled in first while Patsy waits at the porch to be wheeled in. Both her arms are strapped under a blanket, but she still manages to smoke a cigarette.

Edina (*To the driver wheeling her into the ambulance.*) Ow, ow, don't just put me straight in, circle me round a bit. There's nothing worse for people than not seeing the person being put into the ambulance.

Patsy (*Waiting to be wheeled into the ambulance.*) Oi! What about me? I'm sick, too, you know.

scene nine **Exterior hospital. Day three.**

Several photographers and journalists have gathered around the entrance of the hospital awaiting Patsy's arrival. As the ambulance approaches. . .

Journalist Okay, okay, here she comes – MP's tart in mercy dash. That's it, that's it.

Patsy emerges from the ambulance looking glamorous. The photographers crowd around her trying to get her picture. Patsy laps up the attention, while Edina looks fed-up at being completely ignored.

First Photographer Okay, okay.

Second Photographer Patsy, this way – Patsy.

Third Photographer Smile.

Second Photographer Smile this way, Patsy.

Third Photographer Patsy, this way.

Fourth Photographer Patsy . . .

Fifth Photographer Patsy . . . How are you?

Patsy I'm fine. I'm just here with a sick friend.

Journalist Patsy, £10,000 for your exclusive story. D'yer know what I'm saying?

Patsy I regret to inform you that I have already given that exclusive to *Hello* magazine.

Edina How long must I sit here, Patsy?

Patsy I'll send someone out to get you, sweetie.

When she reaches the hospital entrance Patsy poses for the photographers and the cameras click madly.

First Photographer Over here.

Second Photographer How long you in for?

Third Photographer Patsy . . .

Edina (*Pushing her way through the photographers.*) Excuse me I'm sick, I'm sick.

At the entrance of the hospital Edina also poses for a photograph, but the photographers disperse.

scene ten Interior hospital. Day three.

Patsy and Edina look round, checking the room out thoroughly. Edina is in a wheelchair.

Patsy No bloody mini-bar. (*She turns on the TV.*)

Edina Gor! That's hard to credit, isn't it. Really! Oh, let's not have the TV on, darling.

Patsy What is this – morning television?

Edina No, sweetie, it's worse than that. It's mid-morning bloody television, isn't it. Patronising women, castrated males, and Welsh cartoons till people who like a gin and tonic get home at six-thirty, darling. Turn it off.

Patsy turns it off.

Patsy Gin and tonic, Eddy! Ooohh . . .

Edina Oooh! Gin and tonic, sweetie. You order it, sweetie. I'm just going to check out the bathroom.

A nurse comes round with a drugs trolley. She enters the room and looks at Edina.

Nurse (*To Edina, laughing.*) Have you got any pain at the moment dear?

Edina Oh, yes. Yes.

Nurse (*Over her shoulder.*) Mary! Mary! Come in here a minute and look at this.

Another nurse enters.

Mary Mother of God, what is it?

Nurse (*Indicating Edina's outfit.*) You know, my daughter could get away with wearing something like this.

Edina Yes, well, maybe she could get away with it . . . but I doubt very much if she'd be able to afford it.

Nurse Well, she's only three years old.

Edina Oh, God – look, just furnish us with the appropriate drugs and then leave the room, please.

Mary With the laugh you've given us, it's the least we can do for you. Now how about some distalgesic?

Edina Distal . . . Distal . . . Is that all right, Pats?

Patsy Wash them down with brandy.

Edina Yeah, and I want a drip and a little heart-bleep machine. All right? I've seen *Casualty.* I know what goes on.

Mary (*To Patsy.*) Now have you any pain?

Patsy No, but I'm still paying. Have you got any of that stuff they use in *Awakenings*?

Edina El Dopa?

Patsy El Dopa – yes two of those on the rocks and give me some cigarettes.

Nurse Benson and Hedges or Marlboro?

Patsy Both, and bring me the wine list.

They throw cigarettes on to the bed, then start to leave. The first nurse suddenly pauses and goes over to Patsy.

Mary (*To the other nurse.*) Hey – is it her?

Nurse Is it?

Mary Yeah . . . yeah!

Nurse (*In a softer voice.*) Hallo, dear. I thought I recognized you.

Patsy is delighted.

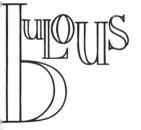

Mary (*To the nurse.*) It's that old slag in the papers last week!

scene eleven Interior hospital. Day four. Edina and Patsy's room.

Edina is in bed. Saffron is near her, but more interested in a TV programme. Patsy is in bed, Fleur and Catriona from the magazine at her bedside. Patsy and guests are all drinking champagne and sorting through freebies spread out on the bed.

Catriona Yes, and then there are these really lovely recherché kilim slippers . . .

Fleur Lovely.

Catriona . . . and chairs I thought might be quite interesting. I've got a friend who's got a shop with some lovely chairs in it.

Fleur Jocasta?

Catriona Yes, and she believes chairs are as important to civilization as a masterpiece or something. I wrote it down somewhere, so we could print that up and do some lovely . . . photos.

Edina (*Pressing the bell for a nurse.*) God, you'd think they'd send a doctor in by now, wouldn't you? I just might be dying here.

Saffron is still engrossed in the TV programme.

Edina Wouldn't you, sweetie? Huh? OI! (*Throwing grapes at Saffron to distract her from the TV.*) Darling, sweetie, visitor . . . visit, visit . . .

Saffron reluctantly sits by Edina.

Edina God . . . She's got two people with her. Two! (*Referring to Patsy.*)

Saffron Those aren't Patsy's friends, are they?

Edina No, darling. They're from the magazine.

Saffron What's she having done? Has she decided yet? It must be hard to find a priority on a face like that.

Edina Sweetie, she's having a little face peel and some eyelid rejuvenation, all right?

Nurse enters.

Edina Oh, God, don't you ever go off duty?

Nurse What do you want?

Patsy Oi – more champagne.

Catriona Can mine be a bucks fizz?

Fleur And some nibbles.

Nurse (*Indicating Saffron.*) Is this your daughter? (*Starts to laugh.*)

Edina Yes.

Nurse Well, maybe there is a God after all. (*Calling.*) Mary!

Edina Don't you dare. Don't you dare. Now, look, I demand to see a doctor.

Nurse Mr Simpson will be round in a minute.

Edina Mr Simpson! Mr Simpson! I want a proper doctor in a white coat who's gonna take me seriously and give me some more painkillers. Now, all right?

Mr Simpson enters.

Mr Simpson Right, Mrs, um, er . . .

Nurse Monsoon.

Mr Simpson I'll be operating on your . . . um, er . . .

Nurse Foot.

Mr Simpson Tomorrow morning.

Edina (*To Saffron.*) Hold my hand, darling. He could be the caretaker for all I know.

Mr Simpson We could do this under local. It's not a very serious operation. It would be very quick.

Edina L . . . L . . . Local? Local anaesthetic? Are you mad? God, what is this Eastern Europe?

Nurse and Doctor exchange glares.

Mr Simpson You wouldn't feel any pain.

Edina I may not feel it, but I'd still be able to see it. I'm not totally lacking in imagination, you know. I want total sensory deprivation and back-up drugs. All right?

Saffron (*To Mr Simpson.*) Believe me, she's much happier unconscious.

Mr Simpson I'll see you tomorrow.

Edina All right?

Mr Simpson Nurse, I know I should see that lumpy-breast woman now, but great friends of mine are having a drinks party . . .

Nurse (*Pointing to Patsy.*) Doctor – the facelift.

Mr Simpson Oh, it'll be a doddle – just grab her by the scalp, shake her up and down a bit and chop off the slack. Tomorrow.

Edina Oi, you! Bitch nurse. (*Nurse pauses.*) Don't you just keep me on the threshold of pain. I want some more painkillers. Look, I had two tiny paraplegics or something in this cup over an hour ago . . . and don't look at me like I'm mad. I know you've got Valium out there.

Fleur (*Picking up face cream.*) Have you tried this? It's a triple-acting alpha hydroxy acid natural complex to reactivate your skin making you scientifically more beautiful.

Catriona Sounds good.

Fleur Dermatologist and opthalmologist tested, non-acne genic . . . I don't know what it means, but it's forcing me to believe it.

Catriona Yes.

Patsy No, I think that's bloody rubbish. You know if you want a face-peel you've got to have the full-strength sulphuric acid skin-stripper. This is a total beauty experience. You know, gnarled old oak

trees have been wheeled into this hospital and gone out as saplings. Look, it says so in the brochure.

Catriona (*Picks up the brochure.*) Breast-enhancement . . . oh, that's an operation?

Fleur Of course, it's an operation.

Catriona Oh, I thought it was just something to do with good lighting.

Fleur All this fuss they're making about implants these days. Breasts have been blown out of all proportion.

Patsy I mean, who wouldn't put up with a not entirely unpleasant trickling sensation and a slight crystallization around the lower abdomen for that amount of cleavage? Uh? Huh-huh?

Magda enters.

Patsy Oh, Magda!

Magda Hallo, Pats. How are you? Unlucky business with the MP. Still, the *Hello!* thing should sort all that out. Right, I'd better make this quick. I've got a lingerie opening and a Feminine wash launch to get to by six o'clock, and all this with my extended working champagne lunch with Anouska-bloody-Hempel floating about here. (*She doesn't pause for breath.*) Right, this month, I want articles about how lovely spending money is, expensive things are better, cosmetics are great, I want money, money, money, spend, spend, spend. I don't want to see any more photos of gormless skeletons with no brains, no make-up and no bloody tits.

Patsy Bored teenagers won't sell a Chanel suit.

Magda Too thin.

Patsy Too young!

Magda If the models get any younger, Pats, they'll be chucking foetuses down the catwalk. All right, we need new photos of everyone, staff, editors and writers to go at the front of the magazine. Stupid bloody idea, but everybody's doing it.

Patsy Oh, I'll get the *Hello!* chap to do a head-and-shoulders of me.

Magda Good. I blame the papers m'self. They started the trend, 'journos with egos'. I don't like them. I mean, it's hard enough to read most of the crap that's written without having to look at a photo of the bastard that wrote it. Right, these are the shots I had done. I don't care what I look like. It's the attitude.

Patsy Oh, Magda – who did these?

Magda Bailey, O'Neill, Lichfield . . . No crap.

Fleur It seems a pity to use just the one. Couldn't we make a feature? 'Our Editor'.

Catriona Yes, and then we could use all these lovely . . . um . . . photos.

Fleur . . . and then each week, do the same with all of us.

Catriona Yes, chairs. Chairs might be nice . . .

Edina (*To Saffron.*) Are you going?

Saffron Yes.

Edina Home?

Saffron No. I'm going to the party at the Halls.

Edina Oh! What, so you won't be here when I come round then?

Saffron For the first time in my life, no.

Edina Oh, right . . .

Saffron picks up her bag, then leans across to kiss Edina goodbye. As she does so a can of low-alcohol cider drops out on to the bed. Edina is astonished. Neither knows what to say.

Saffron (*Snatching it back.*) It's just for the room-warming . . . Look, Mum, just don't be happy, or pleased, or anything.

Saffron rushes out embarrassed. Magda, Fleur, and Catriona exit as nurse brings in tablets. They are talking about how big the articles are going to be about themselves.

ABSOLUTELY fa

Edina (*Looking across to Patsy.*) Huh! You all right, Pats?

Patsy Yeah, darling. You?

Edina Yeah-yeah-yeah-yeah-yeah. Not nervous . . . are you, darling?

Patsy No, not a bit. I can't wait. The day after tomorrow my life begins again. Goodbye ageing obscurity and *Hello* magazine!

Edina throws the sleeping pills down her throat.

Edina God! Oh, it would take more than two of these to knock . . .

She falls back unconscious.

scene twelve Interior operating theatre. Day five. Morning.

Edina is being prepared for the operation, the faces of the doctor and nurses looking over her.

Mary (*To Edina*) Did you take the pre-med?

Nurse She took everything we had! Come on. (*Takes a cigarette out of her hand.*)

Edina (*Struggling.*) No . . . no . . .

Nurse Don't be silly, don't be silly.

Edina I want them . . . (*Nurse takes her earrings off.*)

A bright light is above her and a man in a mask is looking down at her.

Mr Simpson Now count to ten slowly.

Edina One . . . (*Falls back on the pillows.*)

Mr Simpson She's gone.

Nurse Praise the Lord!

Scene fades.

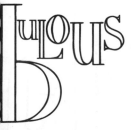

scene thirteen Interior hospital. Day five. Edina and Patsy's room.

As Edina slips under the anaesthetic we fade into her dream. It is in hospital, but the room is dark and unreal. There is a jumble of voices talking that gradually fades down. She slowly begins to focus and we are aware of Lady Penelope sitting on the end of her bed. She stands up and begins to walk up the bed towards Edina.

Lady Penelope Aah. Edina, my dear. It's sad news, I'm afraid. The doctors say there is nothing they can do. Brains is working on the formula, but he may not have enough time. I'm *very* sorry. (*There is a large tear on her cheek.*) Your friends and family are here.

A blonde woman is sitting with her back towards Edina.

Edina Patsy? (*The woman turns around.*) You're Mandy Rice-Davies. Where's Patsy?

'Patsy' (Mandy Rice-Davies) No, sweetie. It's Patsy. This is a dream.

Edina How do I look, Pats?

'Patsy' Wonderful. You never seem to age. I've always been jealous of that.

Edina Huh! It's just bone structure, Pats. My whole body just hangs off these cheekbones.

'Patsy' Don't die, Eddy! You're my touchstone, Eddy.

Edina I think I should see my family now. (*She sees Saffy. It is Helena Bonham-Carter, wearing a Lacroix suit.*) Saff? Saffy, darling. Sweetie, you wore the Lacroix!

'Saffy' (Helena Bonham-Carter) Yeah, I'll always wear my Lacroix from now on. When I'm in town, Mamma. (*Takes Edina's hand.*) Yeah, and I've decided not to go to university.

Edina Good.

'Saffy' I'm going to bum around Europe experimenting with drugs for as long as it's fashionable, and then take a flat in Paris. Just be a famous artist . . .

ABSOLUTELY fa

Edina Yes, darling.

'Saffy' . . . and people will know that I owe it all to you.

Edina Thank you, darling. I know we've had our little ups-and-downs, sweetie, but I will always sort of love you, you know. (*They laugh.*) Is your father here, sweetie. Is Justin here?

'Saffy' Papa's just here, Mamma.

Edina Ah, Justin . . . (*She looks up and sees Richard E. Grant.*)

'Justin' (Richard E. Grant) (*Standing next to Edina's bed.*) You can't die. You wonderful woman, you. I won't let you.

Edina Tell me you're not gay.

'Justin' No, I'm not. I used that as an excuse. When we split up I knew I'd never find another woman to take your place. I didn't want another woman. I shall, of course, be sending a letter to this effect to all those bitch-friends of yours who said 'I told you so'. And it will be in print in the obituary in *The Times*, which they will print by mistake, because I'm sure you're gonna pull through.

Edina Is my son here? Is Serge here? My – my pride and joy?

'Saffron' (Helena Bonham-Carter) Mamma, he's taking weather-readings in the Arctic. Yes, I faxed the North Pole.

They all laugh rather tragically. Edina coughs dramatically.

Richard Oh, my God. Get one of the nurses. Someone must be doing something!

A nurse appears. It is Suzi Quatro.

'Nurse' (Suzi Quatro) Hi, honey. The doctors tried to stop me, but I said you give that chick anything she needs. I'm from Detroit and I don't mess around. Now what do you need? Sex? Drugs? Rock-'n'-roll?

Edina Rock-'n'-roll?

Suzi starts playing guitar and singing.

Suzi (*Singing.*) . . . So make a stand for your man honey. Try to can the can. So put the man in the can honey. Get 'em while you can.

'Nurse' continues singing while . . .

'Justin' Your mother's here.

'Saffron' Yes, Gran is here, Eddy.

Edina Oh! What's she doing here?

She looks over and sees Germaine Greer who comes and sits on the bed.

'Mother' (Germaine Greer) I was just passing, dear. Goodness you're looking young. You hardly seem to have changed since you were a little girl.

Edina You're not looking so bad yourself. In fact, I thought you'd be a lot older.

The dream is beginning to end.

'Mother' It's my bone structure, dear. Your whole body hangs off *my* cheekbones.

'Nurse' is still singing, and by now everyone has joined in.

'Nurse' . . . so come alive . . .

All Yeah . . .

'Nurse' . . . Come alive . . .

All Yeah . . .

Suzi . . . Down in Devil Gate Drive. So come alive . . .

All Yeah . . .

Suzi . . . Come alive . . .

All Yeah . . .

Suzi . . . Down in Devil Gate Down in Devil Gate Down in Devil Gate Drive . . .

Edina (*Trying to kick Lady Penelope off the foot of her bed.*) Get off. Get off.

Scene fades.

scene fourteen Interior hospital. Day five. Post-op.

Edina wakes up. She is back in her room and is kicking a nurse who is trying to put a plaster on her foot. Her mother is there.

Mr Simpson Mrs Monsoon, how are you feeling?

Edina (*Sees Mother.*) Oh, God. What are you doing here?

Mother Well, I was visiting someone from my bridge club, dear, just down the corridor, so I thought as I was passing I might as well just look in . . .

Edina My foot, my foot. I must see the scar. (*She looks. There is a tiny plaster covering the spot.*) Is that it? Huh?

Mr Simpson Yes, it wasn't very much in the end, not even a toe-nail in fact.

Edina Well, what then?

Mr Simpson Well, we removed this. (*Produces an acupuncture needle.*) It's an acupuncture needle. It must have worked its way down.

Edina But I've only ever had cranial acupuncture. Oh! how many organs has it harpooned on its way down there. I'm like a needle-dumping ground. (*To nurse.*) Well, put a bandage on it at least, you. Where's Patsy?

scene fifteen Patsy's dream. Day five. Interior operating theatre.

Patsy is ready for surgery. There are dotted lines drawn under her eyes. She has been anaesthetized, and is woozy.

Patsy Fantastic.

All goes misty as we go into her dream sequence of close-up shots of Hello! *magazine. The pages of the magazine are being turned to reveal perfectly lovely photographs of Patsy in a variety of poses. Antonia's voice is heard reading imaginary copy from the feature, and Patsy's voice is heard graciously responding.*

Antonia (Voice Over) At her tasteful London home, which she decorated herself, I met the lovely internationally renowned fashion model Patsy Stone.

Patsy (Voice Over) I love to collect things. There's nothing I like better than shopping for nick-nacks.

Antonia (Voice Over) Patsy nibbled a humble salad and sipped on Evian water.

Patsy (Voice Over) I like to maintain a healthy lifestyle.

Antonia (Voice Over) It's hard to believe that Patsy is thirty-nine years old. She looks *so* young.

Patsy (Voice Over) Thank you.

Antonia (Voice Over) So young!

Patsy (Voice Over) Thanks.

Antonia (Voice Over) Young!

scene sixteen Interior hospital. Day five.

Patsy slowly comes round. A nurse hands her a mirror.

Nurse Wake up, Miss Stone. The operation is over. A complete success.

Patsy looks into the mirror. She is beautiful – more beautiful than ever.

scene seventeen Interior hospital. Day five. Edina and Patsy's room.

Mother is still there. Edina is watching TV.

Mother I'll just pop in to see poor old Patsy, dear. I think I heard them wheel her back in. (*She knocks on the dividing door.*) Patsy? It's only me. May I come in?

Patsy (Voice Over) Come in, Mrs M. I think you're in for a very pleasant surprise.

Mother enters. She looks at Patsy, is horrified, screams and faints. Patsy's

operation has been a disaster. She has no skin left on her face. Confusion ensues. Patsy grabs a mirror and realizes the full horror. Her dreams of the perfect Hello! *feature are shattered.*

Patsy Oh, no! Sweetie! No! (*Yelling.*) Eddy!

Edina (*Rushes in.*) Oh, God!

Patsy Oh, Eddy-Eddy-Eddy-Eddy-Eddy!

Panic ensues. The nurses try to bring Mother round. They suggest she is admitted to the hospital, but Edina refuses claiming she is not insured and must go to an NHS hospital.

Edina (*To Patsy.*) Darling! (*To nurse.*) Don't leave her here! (*Pointing to Mother.*) NHS! NHS! NHS! Not in *my* bed. NHS.

Patsy sinks back in deep shock.

Credits. Edina and Patsy leave hospital looking much more dignified than when they arrived. Edina is hobbling on crutches and Patsy, wearing dark glasses, has a scarf concealing her face. Neither looks at all happy as they enter the ambulance.

scene eighteen **Interior Edina's kitchen. The following week.**

Patsy is looking better, but not perfect. She and Edina are both drinking. There is the copy of Hello! *magazine open on the table.*

Edina Oh, – never mind, darling.

Patsy Oh. Heigh-ho.

The Hello! *article reads: 'Patsy Stone 49-year-old woman at centre of sex row recovers at friend's home after horrific facelift.' It is a small black-and-white one-page feature with horrible picture of scarred Patsy.*

Edina You're not crying, are you, darling.

Patsy No, sweetie. It's just this little wound under my eye won't heal. The wound this side won't heal either. Huh! Eddy! (*Bursts into tears and throws her head on to the table.*)

ABSOLUTELY ffa

death

Cast List

Edina · JENNIFER SAUNDERS
Patsy · JOANNA LUMLEY
Saffron · JULIA SAWALHA
Mother · JUNE WHITFIELD
Bubble · JANE HORROCKS
Nurse · LLEWELLA GIDEON
Sondra Lorrance · GWEN HUMBLE
Marshall · CHRISTOPHER RYAN
Mark · MARK TANDY
Art Gallery Assistant · NATASCHA TAYLOR
Vicar · CIARAN McINTYRE

scene one Sitting-room. Day one. Night.

The scene opens and we don't know where we are. It feels like a club. There is heavy music, crazy strobe lights. Edina and Patsy are energetically dancing. They are sweaty and drunk.

Patsy Do you want some Ecstasy, Eddy?

Edina Are you mad, darling? Nobody's taking that any more. People have been dragged from 'raves' bleeding from every orifice.

Patsy But this isn't a rave. It's a happening.

Edina Don't force me to take it, Pats. I promised Saffy I wouldn't, darling.

Patsy Yeah, but she'll never find out. Anyway she doesn't scare me.

At that moment the lights are switched on and the music stops simultaneously. We realize it is Edina's sitting-room and Saffron is standing by the door.

Saffron MUM!

Patsy swallows the Ecstasy pills.

Saffron Keep the noise down.

scene two Interior Edina's bathroom. Day two.

Edina is being wrapped in hot-mud bandages head-to-foot like a mummy. She is laid on something like a masseuse table. There is a nurse in beauticians' overalls finishing off the wrap.

Edina A bit tighter round the wrist. Yes, tighter. Well, where's Olive? She normally does me.

Nurse She's sick.

Edina Oh, God. I thought you were a nurse. Why aren't you nursing?

Nurse This pays better. How much are you hoping to lose?

Edina Well, normally I lose about ten inches from all over my body.

Nurse How many times have you had this done?

ABSOLUTELY fab

Edina Seven.

Nurse I'll see what I can do.

Edina Yeah.

Nurse But, personally, I think you're wasting your money. You want to lose weight? (*Answers her own question.*) You want to move your fat bottom and get that mouth sewn up. You want to help the environment? (*Answers her own question.*) Use your fat bottom and plug up the ozone layer.

Edina Are you trained at this?

Nurse I'm a nurse. Bandaging is what I do best. And I've got the manual.

Edina Good.

Nurse Right. Have you recently had or are you due for your period?

Edina Well, yes, both. Why is that important?

Nurse No, I'm just making conversation. Relax.

Saffron enters looking more serious than usual.

Saffron Mum . . .

Edina Oh, what?

Nurse Oh! It's the little daughter.

Saffron Mum – can you come downstairs, please?

Edina Sweetie, have you seen who you're talking to? Tutankhamen.

Saffron Mum, it's important.

Edina Oh, God!

Saffron I've got some bad news.

Edina Darling, I can't move for an hour, I'm being shrunk. And then I've got to go and pick Patsy up from the hospital.

Saffron tuts.

Edina And don't tut her. Do you think she wanted her stomach pumped again? No! She thought they were her antibiotics, darling.

Saffron Gran is downstairs and she wants to see you.

Edina Oh – well, that's never really worked as a threat that one, has it.

Saffron She's got some very *sad* news.

Edina Oh, how tragic! Oh, what? What?

Saffron (*Begins to cry.*) I think she should tell you.

Edina Oh, come on. I'm doing something. Oh, God. What are you blubbing for now?

Saffron Mum! Come downstairs now.

Edina gets up with difficulty and starts to go. Saffron looks at her.

Edina Oh. I'll come, but if I come the Dead Sea comes with me. Is that all right? (*To nurse.*) Is it all right if I move?

Nurse Oh, there you go again, mistaking me for someone who gives a damn. (*She continues as Eddy and Saffron exit.*) Who cares if you're fat or thin? Who cares if you live or die?

scene three **Interior kitchen. Day two. Moments later.**

Mother is there. Saffron and Edina enter. Edina is still in bandages.

Saffron Gran.

Mother (*Cheerfully.*) Good morning, dear. (*Mother sits up, looking through large reading magnifying glass.*) Ooh, I say, is that all the rage?

Edina It's a wrap.

Mother Oh, they've changed since my day. Is it a Vivienne Westwood?

Saffron Gran! (*Puts her arm around her.*) Come on. You've got something to tell Mum, haven't you.

Mother Do we have to?

Saffron Come on, Gran.

Mother Oh ... (*Remembering what it is.*) No, you tell her, dear, you're better at these things. I don't know why, but I have the feeling I might laugh.

Saffron That would just be an hysterical reaction.

Mother Yes, hilarious, dear, but I do think it would be rather inappropriate.

Edina Come on. I mean, does this look comfortable?

Saffron Mum, maybe you should sit down.

Edina No, darling, my crust can't be broken.

Mother You tell her, Saffy.

Saffron No, you tell her, Gran. It'll be all right.

Mother Oh – we could do 'one potato, two potato'.

Edina Just one of you now ... one!

Saffron and Gran then start to speak together.

Saffron/Mother Your ...

Saffron Oh ...

Mother Oh no, dear, all right you say.

Saffron No, after you.

Mother Edina, dear. Your father is dead.

Edina doesn't react.

Saffron Well done, Gran.

Edina Well done? Has she finished him off or something?

Mother (*To Saffron.*) That *was* it wasn't it, dear? I'm not going mad, am I?

Saffron (*Crying.*) Grandad has died. Is that all you can do, all you can say? Don't you think Gran needs a little bit more?

Mother Oh, don't drag me into it, dear. She's doing her best, I'm sure. Now don't you get yourself into a state.

Saffron (*Goes to Edina.*) Your father is dead. What does that make you feel, Mum? And you can stop smirking.

Edina Upset, sweetheart . . . upset, upset.

Mother There I told you, dear.

Saffy goes to hug Edina.

Edina I'm not ready to crack yet.

Mother (*To Saffron.*) Oh, leave the mummy and come to Granny, dear.

Saffron goes tearfully to hug Mother. Edina is jealous.

Edina I *am* upset, darling. (*Tries to pull the right face.*)

Saffron (*Angrily.*) Mum! Just go back upstairs and don't come down until you've really thought about it.

Edina I have thought about it now, darling. I realize . . . Come away from the old woman! Look, Mummy's upset . . .

Saffron Go!

Edina exits.

Mother I don't know how you do it, dear. She would never do that for me.

Saffron (*Trying to be cheerful.*) I expect Grandad kept her in check, though.

Mother Oh, no! He was scared stiff of her.

scene four Interior bathroom. Day two.

Edina is putting herself through a full range of emotions as she has the final bandage removed. The nurse is measuring her.

Nurse These bandages are very clean. Where's all the mud?

Edina Well, is that good?

Nurse I don't know. Get up. Let me measure your wrist. (*Puts a tape-measure around Edina's wrist and looks worried.*) Oh. I don't know how this could have happened. My God, woman, what have you done?

Edina What? What?

scene five Interior kitchen. Same day.

Saffron and Mother are seated. Mother is reading her Take A Break.

Mother This will take your mind off it, Saffy.

Saffron I'm sorry, Gran. You're coping so well. I just feel so sad.

Mother It's all right, dear, I've had longer to get used to the idea of Grandad dying. We were married for nearly forty years, you know.

Saffron It's just there's so much to think about – to arrange.

Mother All in good time. (*Returning to her quiz.*) Now, it's multiple-choice questions. Are you ready? (*Saffron nods.*) How many years was Margaret Thatcher Prime Minister?
a) 900 years
b) 3,000 years
c) 11 years.
Oh, it's a trick question.

Edina enters. She is in a bathrobe and looking very depressed. Saffron goes to her and gives her a hug.

Saffron Oh, Mum, it's all right.

Edina No, it's not all right, is it, sweetie? It's not all right. It's impossible. It just can't have happened, darling . . . Oh . . .

Saffron Do you want to talk about it?

Edina Yeah. I've put on twelve inches all over my body. I mean, my body absorbs mud! Every pore is now an over-eater.

Saffron I don't understand you, Mum.

Edina I'm a medical freak, sweetie.

Saffron gives up.

Mother (*Puzzling over the quiz.*) Of course, they want you to say eleven years and that makes *me* think that it must be 900 years. It was a very very long time ... Oh dear!

Saffron is crying.

Mother Oh, dear!

Edina What's the matter with her? I mean, you know ...

Mother She's upset about your father dying.

Edina What still?

Saffron (*Pulling herself together.*) Look. There are certain things that we should talk about, get sorted out. I mean, like the funeral arrangements, the Will, and also about Gran. I mean, where is she going to live?

Edina/Mother No.

Saffron What?

Edina/Mother She's/I'm not going to come and live here.

Edina No-no-no-no-no!

Mother No-no!

Saffron But ...

Mother No, dear, I'm quite happy where I am. In fact, I'll have a bit more room.

Saffron Are you sure?

Mother Oh, yes, dear.

ABSOLUTELY fab

Saffron Well, I spoke to the funeral directors this morning.

Mother Oh, well done.

Saffron And it's going to be next Monday.

Mother All right, I'll make a note of that. I think I'm free. (*Jots it down in her diary.*) Ooh, cancel bridge!

Saffron And then everyone can come here...

Edina Here?

Saffron (*Shutting Edina up with a look.*) ... and then go to the church.

Edina Yes, well I'm a Buddhist.

Saffron (*Shouting.*) Well, don't come then, don't do anything, don't think about it, don't care!

Silence.

Mother I think I'll be off. (*Kisses Saffron.*) I'll just pop home and sort things out there, dear. Take care and ... thank you. (*She exits.*)

Edina (*Feeling left out.*) Oh, goodbye. Oh, goodbye.

Saffron I can't believe the way you're behaving that you don't care.

Edina I do care, darling ... Did he leave a Will? (*Saffron looks at her horrified.*) What? I'm just asking. You know, asking! I mean, I've made out a Will, you know, darling. I mean, you get most of my money in my Will you know. What do you think you'll do with it, darling, the money?

Saffron I don't want it.

Edina (*Imitating her.*) 'I don't want it'. Well, just don't have it then. I'd rather you didn't have it, in fact. God, it's a rather depressing thought, isn't it, that you might live on after me. Isn't it, um? *You?* Uh? Is that how I'll be remembered is it? Through *you?*

Saffron Well, what do you want? A statue?

Edina Yes.

Saffron A great big, fat, ugly, armless statue?

Edina (*Thinks.*) I've got arms, *I've got arms.* (*Waving arms around.*) I just want to bequeath something to the nation, that's all. Not just you. (*She exits, once again waving her arms around.*)

scene six **Exterior Cork Street. Day two.**

Edina is walking down the street looking in all the windows until she sees something she likes. She enters a gallery.

scene seven **Interior gallery. Day two.**

There are modern pictures and sculptures all around. Very cool refined atmosphere. Very superior assistant.

Assistant Can I help you?

Edina Yeah, I want to buy some art.

Assistant Have you seen something here?

Edina Well, I don't know. I just, you know, I just want to get some you know. What else have you got?

Assistant We're a specialist gallery. Perhaps if you knew what you were looking for I could help you.

Edina Is there someone else who could help me?

Assistant presses a button on her desk. Mark, an expert, appears.

Edina Er, yeah, I want to, you know, buy some art. I'm a collector. I want that sort of modern stuff.

Mark Please come downstairs. We'll see what we can do.

Edina follows him, passing the girl assistant.

Edina (*To assistant.*) You only work in a shop, you know. You can drop the attitude.

scene eight Interior gallery viewing room. Day two.

Mark is bringing in various beautiful pieces and pictures and showing them to Edina. He has a speech that accompanies each piece. He talks about the artistic values and aesthetics. Edina is not impressed.

Mark In this exhibit, notice the quality in the texture of the brushstrokes. We like to think the artist managed to cast off inertia and overcome habit in a continual renewal of himself.

Edina God, look, don't give me all this crap.

Mark I understood you were a collector.

Edina I'm a serious collector. I am not interested in artistic value. I just want to know how much this is going to be worth in twenty years time.

Mark Oh, I see. Why didn't you say so? I've been showing you completely the wrong stuff.

Edina What's this? This? Oh! Why aren't the figures on there? I want to see the figures. (*She is looking at pictures and sculptures that are very modern – the worst of modern collectable art.*) And I like these here, too, these shoes. I like that and those televisions there – I like those. Televisions, those, there – I like those. Also I want one of those, like those bloodheads. You know those frozen bloodheads filled with blood. Anything that's in the Saatchi collection . . . I want things like that, all right? I just want everything, all right . . . everything. I mean, it all looks like bollocks so it must be worth something.

scene nine Interior kitchen. Day two. Night.

It is dark. Edina is in her nightclothes. She goes to the fridge, gets a drink and something to eat, and sits at the table in semi-darkness. Saffron then appears.

Saffron Is that you, Mum? (*Edina nods.*) What are you doing down here in the dark? I heard you get up.

Edina (*Snuffling.*) Oh . . . ho.

Saffron Oh, Mum . . . (*Saffy hugs her.*)

Edina Ooh, well, I suppose it had to hit me sooner or later, darling, didn't it.

Saffron Yes.

Edina Actually, darling, it's made me think, you know.

Saffron Good.

Edina I don't want to die. I mean I don't want to die. I mean, I know you think I don't feel things, you know, and . . .

Saffron I'm sorry we had that row this morning.

Edina That's all right. I've spent most of the money now, by the way, you know.

Saffron I don't care.

Edina You still get the house though, darling. You know that, don't you, and any little keepsake, any little reminder, you want of Mummy when she's passed away, when she's gone, darling. Just say and it shall be yours, you know. Um?

Saffron I can't really think of anything right now.

Edina There must be something. Isn't there something?

Saffron No.

Edina What? Nothing?

Saffron No, nothing.

Edina In the whole place. Nothing? What, not an ashtray? You know, not a piece of cutlery, a glass, something from the fridge? Um?

Saffron Mum, I don't want to think about it.

Edina Yeah, well I don't want to think about it either, but I have to, 'cos I'm dying!

Saffron You're not.

Edina I am. (*She holds out her palm to Saffy.*) Look, look, look at those, darling. Look, look, look. They're stunted.

Saffron You bite your nails.

Edina No, not the nails, darling, my lifelines, my lifelines.

Saffron They look fine.

Edina They end.

Saffron Mum, we all die.

Edina Yeah, well, I don't want to, darling. Honestly when I think of how much I've invested in this body, in this life, darling. I mean, I've had the best of everything. I've been pampered by Champneys, I've been fed by Fortnums, I've been shaved, plucked and moisturized, sweetie. This carcass ain't croaking or I'll sue.

Saffron Look, Mum, if you really want to talk about it perhaps now would be the time to tell me about what you want when you die and what sort of funeral? Where would you like to be buried?

Edina Hang on, I'm not dead yet. Hang on.

Saffron I know.

Edina I don't want to be buried. I don't want to be buried. Have you ever been to a graveyard? Have you ever read a tombstone, sweetie? Hum? You know, 'so and so fell asleep and was buried on date'. *Fell asleep*, sweetie! No, no! No grave for me, darling. I'm a Buddhist anyway, I want to be laid down on a rock in the middle of the Ganges, darling, and just be pecked by birds. I don't want end up as some drugged up zombie in a hospital, all right?

Saffron I thought that would appeal to you.

Edina I want to die with a bit of dignity, you know. I don't want the last words I hear to be 'Switch her off'.

Saffron Mum, I wouldn't!

Edina You wouldn't, would you, darling. (*She sighs deeply.*) Oh, God. 'Life is a mystery. Everyone must stand alone.'

Saffron That's lovely.

Edina 'I hear you call my name and it feels like home.'

Saffron Who said that?

Edina That's Madonna, darling. (*Goes on to sing 'Like a Prayer'.*) 'When you call my name, it's like a little prayer, I'm down on ...'

The door buzzer goes.

Saffron Who can that be? It's three o'clock in the morning.

Edina I don't know. It must be some old drunk or something. You go, you go. (*Saffron exits.*) 'Little prayer, I'm down on my knees, I want to ...' (*She gets a large bulldog clip and puts it on her hand to try and crease up her lifeline a bit.*) Come on, live, live.

Saffron re-enters followed by Patsy.

Saffron You were right. I'm going to bed.

Saffron exits. Patsy is standing looking pissed-off.

Edina What are *you* doing here?

Patsy You were supposed to collect me, Eddy.

Edina What?

Patsy From the hospital. I was waiting. (*She coughs up a still-attached tube.*)

Edina I'm sorry, darling, you know, it's just that ... Well, we've had some rather bad news today, that's all.

Patsy I need a drink.

Edina It's very bad news actually, Pats.

Patsy Oh, what?

Edina I'm dying.

Patsy You can't ...

Edina Well, I am.

Patsy Well, what am I supposed to do, if you die?

Edina Get cabs!

ABSOLUTELY fa

scene ten Interior kitchen. Day three.

Mother and Saffron are sitting making out a list.

Mother I think that's enough people, dear.

Saffron It's not very many.

Mother I know. I was always telling him to get out more and meet people.

Edina and Patsy enter. Eddy is wearing sad-looking dress, with a sad look on her face. Patsy is in the same outfit as the night before.

Mother Oh, I see, she's in mourning at last.

Saffron Only for herself.

Edina Morning.

Patsy Morning Mrs M.

Mother Good morning, Patsy.

Patsy (*Awkwardly.*) Um . . . Eddy tells me that Mr M . . . you know . . . dead.

Mother That's right.

Patsy Well . . . um . . . I . . . condole you.

Mother Thank you, dear.

Patsy He chose the right season to go.

Saffron What do you mean?

Patsy Well, Harvey Nics have got some really tasty little black numbers at the moment. And black is like 'in', so you wouldn't have to wear it only the once. (*Saffron tuts.*)

Patsy No, it's my job to know these things.

Edina (*Stroking Saffy's hair and looking at the list on the table.*) Look at the silky sheen on your hair, silky sheen, silky sheen. What are you doing, silky sheen? What are you doing here, here?

40
41

Saffron Making a list of family and friends for the funeral.

Edina Family? Family? God, I hope you're not inviting that bloody-bollocky, selfish two-faced, chicken bastard pig-dog man, are you? Um? Um?

Saffron You could just say Dad, I'd still know what you meant. Anyway, he can't come, he's away.

Edina Oh, good.

Saffron And Marshall can't make the funeral either. He's flying back to LA tomorrow, but he might call in this morning to pay his respects.

Mother How kind.

Edina Oh, no.

Patsy Not with that bitch girlfriend.

Saffron He's got a new one.

Edina Oh, no!

Saffron She's a therapist.

Patsy Let's get out of here, Eddy.

Door buzzer goes.

Edina Damn. The window . . . the window.

Edina and Patsy rush for the window.

Saffron Stay!

Patsy and Edina freeze.

Mother (*Admiringly.*) You've done it again, dear.

scene eleven Interior kitchen. Day three. Short while later.

They are all seated around the table. Eddy, Patsy, Saffron, Mother, Marshall and Sondra Lorrance, his new girlfriend. She would like to think she is 'Annie Hall' but is really rather styleless and straight. She has a small

notebook constantly at hand, and a look on her face that is rather patronizing and is saying 'I think I know what you are thinking, and what you are about to say, and why you're saying it'. She is reading aloud from a book; everyone is bored. This has obviously been going on for a while.

Sondra We are but mere ghosts, we are spirits soaring. For some say forsooth that we die at our conception and will then henceforth be reborn into vibrant life when we truly pass on. For herewith, I say to you, who can say, whether we are alive or already dead.

Marshall That's enough now, Sondra.

Sondra (*To Mother.*) Oh, I'd like you to have this. You dear recently bereaved one. Oh, I hope you don't mind me terming you so. There's a passage in the book that relates to that actually. (*Opens book again.*)

Edina Marshall! (*Gives him a look to stop her.*)

Marshall Sondra, that's enough, honey.

Sondra Oooh, just this little bit . . .

Edina Oh, no!

Marshall Can I have a drink?

Mother Oh, what a good idea.

Saffron Are you drinking again?

Marshall Yeah.

Patsy Welcome back, Marshall.

Marshall Thanks, Patsy.

Edina I suppose you're no good to her unless you have a problem.

Marshall How perceptive.

Sondra (*Reading.*) I am not what others perceive me to be. I am not what I am called, I am not a name. I am my own invention.

42

43

ABFAB

Edina Oh!

Saffron I've heard that before somewhere. It's Jung or . . .

Sondra (*Defensively.*) No, it's a traditional quote. I am merely using the meaning. No credit required. You can check it out with my lawyer. Here.

Mother Did you write this, dear?

Sondra Yeah. That's me, Sondra Lorrance. I think the title says it all, don't you? *Hey, It's Great To Grieve!*

Saffron So, Marshall. How's the script coming?

Edina Oh, no, do we have to know?

Marshall Well, it's at a real interesting stage . . . (*Looks to Sondra for reassurance.*)

Sondra You're doing just fine.

Marshall We had Keanu Reeves pull out, which . . . which . . . (*Looks to Sondra.*) . . . we feel really positive about now because it has taken a different course entirely and a Japanese company has taken up the option to do it in animation form.

Sondra Pat yourself on the back for that.

Edina A cartoon!

Patsy A cartoon!

Marshall Animation.

Edina A cartoon! (*Laughs.*)

Edina and Patsy are still laughing, as Sondra turns to talk to Edina.

Sondra Hi, you really interest me. I'd really like to talk to you. Now, don't worry, I'm a therapist. I'm Gestalt.

Patsy (*Trying to exit.*) And I'm g-going. Let's go, Eddy.

Edina Yeah, I'm going too. Saff, I'm out of here, and then I'm going to change and have lunch with Pats.

ABSOLUTELY fa

Sondra (*To Edina.*) You really are very aggressive to her. (*Indicating Saffy.*) Do you perhaps feel that you blame and hold your daughter responsible for ageing, for your loss of looks?

Edina No. What's your excuse?

Edina and Patsy leave. There is a silence broken by Sondra.

Sondra (*Taking a deep breath.*) Ummmmm. That was a quality moment.

Mother Oh, good.

Sondra I, too, have felt great sadness. You are talking to someone who has sat through *Beaches* twelve times.

Mother Really?

Buzzer goes.

Mother Oh, that'll be Grandad.

Sondra Oh! How sweet. You still think he's coming home.

Saffron No, it really is Grandad. Er . . . we're putting the coffin in the sitting-room so that people can come and pay their respects.

Sondra (*Total disbelief.*) Excuse me, would you run that one by me again? Um? The coffin . . . Am I right?

Saffron Yes.

Sondra With the . . .

Marshall Careful, honey.

Mother With the body, yes.

Sondra (*Hysterically.*) Body. What are you crazy? Body?

Marshall Calm down, calm down . . .

Sondra Honey, these people are crazy. You can't put a body a . . .

Marshall Calm down, calm down, calm down, *calm down* . . .

Sondra . . . it's gonna smell – it's gonna smell so bad!

Marshall Just calm down. It's all right.

Sondra (*Screaming.*) Honey – take me home!

scene twelve Exterior Edina's house. Day three.

Edina and Patsy are driving towards the house. There is a hearse parked right outside. Edina pulls up.

Patsy Do you think the Yankee bimbo from hell's gone?

Edina God, I hope so, darling. (*They get out of the car, and walk up to the house, Edina spots the hearse.*) Oi! Private parking. I park here, you have to have a permit.

scene thirteen Interior sitting-room. Day three.

Various pieces of modern art have been placed around the room. The coffin with Edina's father in it is in the room. It is open. Edina and Patsy come into the hallway.

Edina (Voice over) What are you doing here?

Mother (Voice over) Just finalizing arrangements for tomorrow.

Edina (Voice over) Why – what's tomorrow?

Mother (Voice over) It's the funeral.

Edina Come on, Pats. Let's see if my art has arrived? (*Edina and Patsy enter the room and Edina sees art.*) Oh, yes, good. Some smaller bits are here. That bit's here.

She indicates various bits of art, including the coffin.

Patsy (*Looking around.*) Are you mad?

Edina Well, you don't have to like it. That's not the point, darling.

Patsy Well, how much did this lot set you back?

Edina Well, I just spent as much as I could. It cost me hundreds of thousands of pounds.

ABSOLUTELY fa

Patsy Oh, well, in that case it's fabulous, Eddy.

They wander around the room. The coffin is in the foreground, but they do not notice it. They are looking at various bits of 'Art', and Edina is presenting the art as if in a gallery.

Edina I mean, yeah, I have bought the future here, darling. Look, let me show you . . . look . . . look . . . look at this, darling. This bit here . . . This, darling, here.

Patsy Yep.

Edina This is art brute – wood against wall, darling. This is arte poveri – jars darling. Jars.

Patsy Fantastic.

Edina Now, over here, we've got this . . . materialization of the pyschotic's dream deciphered by a clairvoyant . . . Hangers – it's hangers – hangers – and this bit over here. (*Patsy and Edina then cross by the coffin and, suddenly noticing it, stand frozen with fright, staring at it. Edina then continues her presentation.*) This is a sort of . . . This is a corpse in an . . . oaken, open oblong, coffin . . . silky . . . It's a dead body, Pats.

Patsy Yeah, but is it 'art', Eddy?

Edina (*With sudden realization.*) No, sweetie. It's my father.

Patsy Are you sure?

Edina Yeah, I think so. I've never seen him in a suit before. I mean . . .

There are voices from the hallway. Sondra, Marshall, Saffron and Mother appear.

Marshall (Voice over) No.

Sondra (Voice over) No, I want to try one more time.

The door opens and Mother, Marshall and Saffron enter. Sondra is trying to pluck up courage to enter. She is hysterical and takes a large swig from a bottle.

Mother Come along, then.

After much deliberation and hysterical laughter Sondra eventually walks slowly towards the coffin. She just manages to look into the coffin before passing out.

Sondra Oooh-ho-ho! (*She faints.*)

Marshall She wasn't ready.

Mother Oh, dear.

Marshall All right, all right, let's go home. Come on, come on, come on, let's go home.

They pick up Sondra and take her out. Mother picks up a red nose that Sondra was holding and places it on her late husband's chest.

Mother There, Daddy.

Mother exits. Edina and Patsy stand alone staring at the body.

Patsy He looks like he's out of it, Eddy.

Edina They can't just leave him here like this. He just looks so sort of . . .

Patsy Plonked.

Edina I know. I mean he should be against white. It should be back-lit. I mean, no one's thought about it at all, have they?

scene fourteen Sitting-room. Day four.

Saffron and Mother are standing with a group of mourners.

Edina (*Entering, and saying to everyone.*) Cheer up.

Mother I really think we should all be off.

Edina (*Horrified to see her art objects have been abused, and coats have been hung on the coat-hanger mobile.*) Has no one got any respect? Do not touch the art. What you don't seem to realize is that no one would care if you lot were all run over by a bus, but if one piece of this art gets damaged several Lloyds' underwriters go homeless. Is that understood?

Nobody pays any attention to her.

Saffron Come on, Gran, let's get going. (*Takes her arm.*)

Mother Yes, dear, I've got to change my shoes.

Edina watches them all file past her.

Saffron (*To Edina.*) You're not going to the church, are you?

Edina Not unless I'm asked nicely, darling.

Saffron Don't come – or to the cemetery.

Edina Well, I've rung Bubble and asked her to represent me, darling.

Saffron Good.

scene fifteen Interior sitting-room. Day four. Later.

Edina is sitting alone on the sofa with a glass of wine in her hand. She is morose.

Edina (*To herself.*) I might want to go, I might want to go, you know.

Patsy enters with an open bottle of wine. She is slightly drunk.

Patsy Hallo, Eddy.

Edina Hallo, Pats.

Patsy Are you are all right, darling?

Edina Yeah, are you all right, darling?

Patsy Yeah, well, you know. Um, you know . . .

Edina What? What? What?

Patsy . . . Well, well, er . . .

Edina What? What?

Patsy You know, you know. You know you said the other day that you were gonna die.

Edina Yeah, well I might not be now. I'm looking into it you know.

48
49

Patsy Yeah, well – well . . .

Edina Well, what? What, what, what, what?

Patsy No-no-no. Shut up, Eddy. This isn't easy for me.

Edina Sorry, darling.

Patsy It's just that if you were gonna die, I would be . . . like totally alone, you know. I wouldn't have anybody or anything. You know, you've always been the lucky one, Eddy. You've got a family, you've got a great place to live.

Edina Yeah, I've got a great place to live, yeah.

Patsy Even that bitch daughter must be some kind of comfort to you.

Edina Yeah, not always though, not always.

Patsy Yeah, not like a dear friend.

Edina No, not like a friend.

Patsy You know, you've always been a great friend to me, Eddy. I'd miss you.

Edina Would you? You would, wouldn't you. You would.

Patsy Yeah, and I'd . . . I'd . . . I'd like something to remember you by if you were, you know, God forbid, to die.

Edina Yeah, yeah – of course, darling. You can have something you know.

Patsy Yeah, yeah well, I've always been your greatest, you know your best friend, and your protector. (*In a sudden rush.*) Can I have the house?

Edina Oh, Pats! Oh, darling! I was gonna give that to Saffy. Saffy was gonna have the house!

Patsy Yes, well, Saffy doesn't want it. She's not here.

Edina Oh, all right, all right.

Patsy (*Greatly relieved.*) Oh, thanks, Ed.

Edina She's not here, is she. She's not here, and I'm just here . . .

Patsy She's not.

Edina All alone, being sad, all alone.

Patsy Sad. You're just making all these little wrinkles on your face, and *she's* not here.

Edina Yeah, I've got wrinkles. I mean, what's the point of grieving if there's no one there to see you do it?

Patsy You're right, Eddy. You're always right, sweetie.

Edina I'm always right. I mean I should be there, you know. He would want me to be there, wouldn't he, wouldn't he, wouldn't he?

Patsy He'd want you to be there.

Edina (*Jumping up.*) He would want me to be there.

Patsy Yeah.

Edina (*Noticing Patsy has not moved yet.*) He'd want you to be there, as well.

Patsy (*Not moving.*) No, I don't think he'd want me to be there, Eddy.

Edina If you want the house, darling . . .

Patsy (*Quickly getting up and starting to grieve.*) Yeah, he'd want me to be there.

Edina He'd want you there, he'd want you there. Come on, darling, come on.

scene sixteen **Exterior cemetery. Day four.**

Mother, Saffron and Bubble, and a collection of very old men and women are standing by the graveside with a vicar. The ceremony is nearly over and the coffin has been lowered into the grave. Edina's car arrives. Patsy gets out of one side and walks round to open the door for Eddy. Patsy is obviously very drunk and staggering.

50

51

Patsy Get out, Eddy.

Edina flops out of the car on to the ground. They pull themselves together and start trying to walk towards the graveside where the vicar is ending the funeral service. Saffron looks furiously at Edina and Patsy. Mother is indifferent. They stagger getting closer and closer. Edina is slightly ahead of Patsy. Patsy falls into a nearby open grave. Edina ploughs on getting closer and closer. Putting on a final spurt she makes it to the graveside where all are gathered, but can't stop herself and plunges down on top of the coffin.

Mother She's very upset, you know.

Saffron is speechless with anger.

Credits.

scene seventeen Exterior cemetery. Day four. Moments later.

Mother, Saffron, Bubble and others are walking away from the grave. Behind them we see Edina and Patsy trying to climb out.

Edina Oh, help me, sweetie . . .

Mother Let's hope someone fills them in before they get help.

morocco

Cast List

Edina · JENNIFER SAUNDERS
Patsy · JOANNA LUMLEY
Saffron · JULIA SAWALHA
Bubble · JANE HORROCKS
Uncle Humphrey · JOHN WELLS
Yentob · HARROUN HANIF

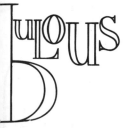

scene one Interior Edina's kitchen. Day one.

Saffron is sitting at kitchen table. Edina enters carrying a small carrier bag and flops down at the table.

Edina Oh, sweetie. Oh, darling. Oh, God, sweetie. What a day. (*Struggling to get Saffy's attention.*) What a day I've had, sweetie darling, darling, darling, sweetie. I have been at work since I left here this morning.

Saffron Do you want some lunch?

Edina No, no lunch. I had a four-course sit-down at the studio . . . the studio, sweetie, the studio, studio, darling. Action! Lights! Camera!

Saffron What have you been doing?

Edina Pop-Specs ad.

Saffron What?

Edina Well, you know I represent Pop-Specs, darling? We're doing a new ad. We're up-marketing the image.

Saffron What are Pop-Specs?

Edina What are Pop-Specs? Are you dead? Are you dead? (*Holding up a pair. They are dark glasses with lenses that pop in and out so you can change style.*) Look, these are them. These are them. Look, darling. These are Pop-Specs. They're great. Look . . . Pops in and out you see, darling. D'you see that one? Another one. Look at this . . . another one, darling. Schizophrenic. They're fantastic.

Saffron How can you up-market those?

Edina Patsy's agreed to put them in a fashion shoot for her magazine and there's the new ad, darling, new ad, which was mainly my idea, my original idea. It's very clever. It had better bloody work. Otherwise, you know my company's gonna be left with one minor department store, two student designers, Smunchie bars and Lulu paying for your upkeep, darling. And Lulu's like that, sweetie. (*Uses hand to show that Lulu's a bit dodgy.*) You could show a little enthusiasm, you know.

Saffron Mum, why should I be happy that you're going to spend thousands of pounds . . . ?

Edina Hundreds of thousands of pounds.

Saffron . . . persuading people to buy some cheap bit of plastic junk that they don't even want . . .

Edina . . . don't know they want yet, sweetie . . .

Saffron . . . for things that will then be thrown away in a matter of months once the novelty wears off and will sit around polluting the planet.

Edina Oh, that's it. That's it, is it?

Edina (*Fumbling for Pop-Specs bag.*) Can I, can I show you something, sweetie? Can I show you something on this? (*Triumphantly.*) Look at that. (*Points to a little sticker on the Pop-Specs bag.*) What do you think that is there?

Saffron (*Unimpressed.*) It's a sticker with a green tree on it.

Edina Yes.

Saffron What does it mean?

Edina (*Triumphantly.*) Kind to trees, sweetie!

The door buzzer sounds. Edina crosses room to push entry button.

Saffron How are they kind to trees?

Edina Well, they ain't made of wood. How kind do you want?

Patsy (*Entering.*) Oh, what a day! A long, tedious day.

Saffron It's two o'clock.

Edina I've been at work all day, too, Pats.

Patsy Well, you're a fool. Still heigh-ho. Now, have you sorted Marrakech? Have you telephoned Humphrey?

Edina Yeah, yeah, we can stay in his villa.

Patsy Fantastic!

Saffron Marrakech? Why are you going to Marrakech?

Edina Well, for the fashion shoot, sweetie.

Saffron Why do you have to go there?

Edina Oh, God. Who are you? Magnus Makerson all of a sudden? Hands on buzzers – 'I don't know. Pass'. Just because . . . all right!

Patsy No, Eddy. Eddy, not 'just because'. This is my job. I mean, these things aren't decided at random.

Edina Yeah. No-no-no.

Saffron It's supposed to be really beautiful out there.

Edina Well, you know, darling, we spent all those Christmases out there, don't you remember, when you were a child?

Saffron You never took me. You always left me here with Gran.

Edina I know but, you got the postcards, didn't you!

Saffron I'm studying the indigenous people of that particular region of Northern Africa for my anthropology module at college this term.

Edina (*To Patsy.*) Do you want some Bolly, darling?

Patsy Yeah, just a smidge.

Saffron It would be really great to be able to go there and study.

Edina Study? You don't go to Marrakech to study . . .

Patsy (*Catching on.*) No, you certainly don't.

Edina You go to Marrakech for . . . I don't know . . . drugs, dirt-cheap plates and rugs . . .

Patsy Yeah . . . easy-going sex with gorgeous under-age youths . . .

Edina Yeah . . . sex changes, wasn't it, Pats? (*Gets a look from Patsy.*) Well, not now, not now. So, darling, you don't go there for studying some ingenuous peasants for an anthology molecule.

Saffron It would really help with my course . . .

Patsy No, no, no.

Edina (*Bewildered.*) What?

Saffron Well, Mum could I . . . ?

Patsy No, Eddy.

Edina What?

Patsy No to whatever she's going to say.

Saffron I'm talking to my mother.

Patsy Just say no, Eddy.

Edina Well, what? What?

Patsy Just tell her no, Eds.

Saffron Please . . .

Edina Well, I don't understand . . .

Saffron Let me go to Morocco.

Patsy No.

Edina (*Relieved.*) Well, why not? Let her go to Morocco . . . We're going to Marrakech!

Saffron That is Morocco, Mum.

Patsy This little scud-from-hell is trying to slime her way on to our trip, and we don't want her.

Saffron But Mum . . .

Patsy Don't you 'but mum' her. You snivelling piece of tripe – you walking enema – we want to have fun, Eddy. We don't want her – no, no, no. You can forget it, babe.

Saffron (*To Edina.*) You're always saying I should go to all these places – it would be good for me. Please Mum – just this once I'm doing something you would like me to do. Please – I wouldn't be in the way.

Edina (*Torn.*) (*To Saffron.*) Look, just do whatever you want . . .

Patsy Eddy!

Edina Well, but as your mother, I take no responsibility for your well-being, all right. You come with us, you're on your own. (*She moves away and turns her back to Saffy and Patsy.*)

Saffron (*Shrieking with pain.*) Ow!

Edina (*Bewildered.*) What?

Saffron (*Pointing to Patsy.*) She burnt me with her cigarette.

Patsy Accident.

scene two Interior Edina's hallway. Day two.

They are nearly ready to leave for the airport. Bubble is standing in hallway with headphones on, singing along to 'There's no Limit . . .' The batteries are erratic so she sings in different speeds.

Edina Listen, Bubble, Bubble, Bubble, darling, please. I need to sort out the Pop-Specs business before I go.

Saffron Mum, we're going to be late. Have you switched everything off upstairs?

Edina Yes.

Saffron I'll check . . . (*Goes upstairs.*)

Patsy (*To Edina.*) Quick, let's go before she gets back.

Edina (*To Patsy.*) No, stay, stay, stay. (*To Bubble.*) Now listen, darling. You've got to get the information, the figures and things to them by next week, all right?

Bubble Yeah. (*Tapping her side as if she has a bag.*) It's right here . . . (*Realizing it isn't.*) Oh!

Saffron (*Coming downstairs. To Edina.*) You left the shower . . . and some bubbling mush on . . .

Edina That's bikini-wax, darling. It's for you, unless you're happy with those sideburns on your inner thighs.

Above Goodbye ageing obscurity, and hello magazine.

Top Patsy is visited.

Middle Edina's dream family – a fabulous celebrity selection.

Above 'It's like a needle dumping ground.'

Above 'Look! He chose the right season to die in.'

Right 'It's not a "rave", it's a happening.'

Opposite 'My crust cannot be broken.'

Above 'It's a corpse,
but is it art?'

Right The living dead.

Opposite 'Help mamma,
sweetie.'

Below 'This is the wall.'

Bottom Shopping.

Above 'It only lasted a year, then it fell off.'

Left A dirty old man.

Above 'Just dig a hole.'

Right **A** whole population screaming out for good quality, reasonably priced kids' casuals.

Saffron Come on, let's go.

Patsy (*To Edina.*) She's not travelling Club, is she?

Edina No, Economy. Practically cargo. (*To Bubble.*) But you've been keeping all the information. Now, you have got the information, haven't you?

Bubble Most of it, yeah, oh yeah, until the special thing broke.

Saffron (*Worried about being late.*) Mum!

Edina Well, hang on ... What thing?

Bubble The thing that's attached to the typewriter. Little animal with a ball.

Edina What animal?

Bubble Little animal. Small ... Creeps about ... Not a rat ...

Patsy A gerbil?

Saffron A squirrel? Hedgehog?

Edina No, no, don't panic her, or we'll never get anywhere. Mouse?

Bubble Yeah, the mouse that's got a telly with VD.

Edina All right, the VDU. The word processor?

Bubble Yeah ... That fell off the table when I took the mouse home.

Patsy Come on, I'm running to a tight schedule. I've got customs, carnet and a meeting in the Clipper Class Cocktail Lounge in forty minutes.

Edina Hang on, hang on, I'm coming ... this is important. You broke the computer?

Bubble Yeah.

Edina When?

Bubble Who can say?

Edina Oh, God. Now listen here, you bloody brainless bimbo. I *need* this client. (*Bubble thinks she is talking to Saffy, and keeps wagging her* *finger at her.*) I don't need some bollocky vegetable yankie-bloody-doodle to mess it up for me, all right.

Saffron (*To Bubble.*) She's talking to you.

Bubble Oh!

Saffron (*To Edina.*) Have you got everything?

Edina Yes, yes got everything. (*She exits, then rushes back in a panic.*) Tickets! Money! Passport! Tickets! Money! Passport!

scene three Interior airport, Marrakech. Day two.

Patsy, Edina and Saffy are lined up by the luggage carousel. It is chaotic.

Patsy Where's the photographic equipment?

Edina God, where's the Pop-Specs bag? Where's the luggage?

(*Their guide Ali appears.*)

Ali I'm sorry the equipment must have gone to Tangiers . . . and the rest . . . I don't know.

Edina (*Spots Pop-Specs bag and climbs on to luggage conveyor belt.*) Pop-Specs!

Saffron Mum!

Edina (*Goes through to the loading bay on the conveyor belt, then reappears.*) Help Mummy, my darling . . .

Saffy spots her own rucksack coming through behind Edina.

Saffron Mum! That's my bag.

Edina picks it up and chucks it back down the shoot so Saffy can't get it.

Edina (*Shouting.*) Unclaimed!

Patsy (*Also climbing on to the belt.*) It's all right. It's all right, Ed. Just a minute.

Patsy and Edina end up being carried away in opposite directions. The scene fades to exterior at the airport.

Patsy Oh leave them. They can sort it out.

They begin exit from the airport.

Edina (*To Saffron who is sulking about her rucksack.*) Take that look off your face. I've got enough stuff here you can borrow.

Saffron I'd rather wear a yashmak.

Patsy That can be arranged.

Edina Now, just get in a cab and go, sweetie. (*As they start to leave the airport building.*) Now prepare yourself for the heat . . . You're not used to . . .

The doors open, the heat hits them. Patsy and Edina pass out.

scene four Exterior villa. A crowded Marrakech street. Later the same day.

60
61

The car pulls up outside the villa.

Saffron Wake up, Mum. We're here.

Edina (*Falls out of the car.*) Where? I am never going anywhere ever again.

Saffron Shut up. Come on.

Patsy emerges and staggers into villa behind Saffy and Edina.

scene five Interior villa. Day two. Later.

Edina and Patsy enter. They are showered and refreshed. Saffy is sitting there. Beside the sofa there is something resembling a pile of old laundry.

Edina Fantastic shower? Has anyone seen Humphrey? (*To Moroccan houseboy.*) Humphrey est here? Humphrey est here? (*Taking drink from tray and a joint from Patsy.*) Thank you, darling. (*To Saffron.*) Do you want some of this, darling? Would you like some of this, sweetie? (*Offers the joint to Saffy.*)

Saffron (*Disgusted.*) No, thank you.

Edina It's all legal here, so you can't disapprove. In fact, it's compulsory, darling. They bust you for not having one of these dangling out of your mouth here. I mean . . . look, we've only been here a couple of hours and already Pats has got some stuff.

Patsy (*Taking joints from her hair.*) No, actually I brought these with me, Eddy.

Edina Oh!

Patsy (*Inhaling deeply.*) This is the life, eh Eddy?

Edina Yeah, this is the life. God, it's all coming back to me now, darling. The noise, the smell . . .

Patsy Yeah, it's like everything's on heat.

Edina Yeah. (*Looks around.*) Remember that sofa and those tiles.

Patsy Oh, gorgeous.

Edina Do you know something – you can't get those tiles for love or money in Fired Earth any more, you know, even in Holland Park, darling. I mean it's ridiculous, it's ridiculous, and over here they're just hanging around on people's walls.

Patsy Yeah, even on peasant's walls.

Saffron Tut–tut–tut–tut.

Edina Sweetie, we dragged these people screaming into the twentieth century. We gave them all the mod-cons, darling. We gave them the non-squat toilet, toilet tissue, darling. I mean how do you think they used to wipe their bottoms before we came along . . . ?

Patsy Old bits of hoof.

Edina Now, they can't even be bothered, sweetie, to send us a few cracked old craft tiles. Well, I'm fed up of it. I'm fed up of it. Are you going to change?

ABSOLUTELY fa

Saffron I haven't got anything.

Edina I thought Patsy offered you the shoot clothes.

Patsy Well, as long as she shaves her scabby armpits and doesn't sweat over everything.

Saffron (*Indicating what she is wearing.*) I'll wash these.

Edina Oh, wash these! With your travel wash! Well, if you could try to look a little less like a Christian missionary I'm sure we'd all be a lot safer. They're all Muslin round here you know, darling.

Edina and Patsy exit to courtyard.

scene six Exterior villa. Courtyard by pool. Night.

Edina and Patsy are admiring the night sky and the stars. They are stoned.

Edina Oh, wow, darling! Look at those stars.

Patsy Yeah...

Edina I mean, it's like talcum powder, isn't it, or something. It's as if it just goes on forever ... or something ... out there.

Patsy (*Spotting a shooting star.*) Oh! Shooting star. (*Points.*)

Edina Where? Where? Where? Where? Where? Where? Where? Where? Where?

Patsy No ... It's, er ... It's gone.

Edina Well, next time you see it, say it quicker – just say it quicker.

There is a scream and shout for help from Saffy.

Saffron Mum! Mum, help me ... Mum!

Edina Oh, what?

Saffron (*Screaming.*) Mum...

Edina and Patsy amble back to the house.

Interior villa. Day two. Night.

Edina and Patsy enter and stand by the doorway looking in. Saffron is being molested by Uncle Humphrey.

Edina What's happening?

Patsy She's being humped by some laundry . . .

Saffy rolls on to the floor and Humphrey stands up.

Edina (*Recognizing the assailant.*) Humphrey! Darling!

Humphrey (*Getting off Saffron.*) Good Lord, I didn't see you there. Oh . . . (*Indicating Saffron.*) I'm so sorry about that . . .

Edina That's all right. It's only Saffy.

Patsy Humph!

Humphrey Oh, Patsy! It's just I've had a couple of drinks and from behind . . .

Patsy Is the only way she'll ever stand a chance.

Humphrey (*To Saffron.*) Very embarrassed, my dear thing.

Saffron It's okay, really.

Humphrey I hope you didn't think I was some sort of dirty old man . . .

Saffron (*Embarrassed.*) No, not at all . . .

Humphrey Oh, good. because that would never do. (*Lasciviously.*) I say you're like your mother . . . (*To the houseboy.*) Er bardo elle machaleyaha. Thank you, Yentob. (*To Saffron.*) Now, would you like to try a little local speciality?

Saffron Oh, yes, I'd love to . . .

Humphrey Well, you take a pot of scented honey, mixed with goat cheese yoghurt sprinkled with almonds from the Atlas Mountains. Spread it all over your naked nubile young body and allow a man old enough to be your father to lick it off . . .

Saffron, horrified, rushes out.

Humphrey Just like her mother . . . Tease, tease, tease.

scene eight Interior villa. Day two. Night.
Later.

They are drinking and smoking joints. Edina is trying to get Saffy stoned.

Edina (*To Saffron.*) You feeling all right, sweetie? Are you all right?
Um? Um? Eat up your cake . . . Eat up your little cake.

Saffron eats cake, which is obviously drugged.

Edina You know, I'm sorry you got off to such a bad start with
Humphrey, darling, but he's really very nice you know. He's a very
good chap, you know.

Humphrey (*To Patsy.*) Cigar, old man?

Patsy Oh thanks, old boy.

Edina (*To Saffron.*) You know, sweetie, when we first came here it
was so beautiful. It was just like a little, a tiny-little-little oasis, darling,
here. Weeny little one.

Patsy Yeah. With like a town.

Humphrey With a couple of quite decent five-star international
hotels with a jacuzzi.

Patsy Oh, yeah, and an airport.

Edina Yeah, all right, all right, all right. I'm just trying to be poetic.

Saffron I'm studying the indigenous population of the area. The
tribes . . .

Humphrey You won't find many of those left . . . the Guinesses, the
Thyssens . . . All gone. Them and Princess Margaret are just a distant
memory.

Saffron I meant the Berbers.

Humphrey (*Puzzled.*) The Berbers? I don't remember them. Perhaps they're an American couple . . . I think I remember them at a cocktail party. You see, the reason people came no longer exists. You know . . . I mean you can get everything you want here anywhere else much cheaper.

Edina (*Knowingly.*) Safer, eh Pats?

Saffron What?

scene nine Flashback 70s Marrakech – Patsy used to be a man.

The villa. A collection of hippies and aristocrats standing around. Some evil-looking Moroccans. Edina dancing with scarf. Humphrey joining in. Man has his back to us.

Edina Come on, darling. Sing.

Humphrey Yes, come on, Pat, old chap.

The man turns around. It is Patsy.

Patsy All right, let's do that Sonny and Cher number. (*Singing.*) 'They say we're young . . . They say we're young.' Oh . . . Hang on, I'll just get this chord right.

Edina 'They say we're young and we don't know . . . La-la-la-la . . .'

Scene fades back to modern-day interior of the villa.

Humphrey Do you want a brandy, old chap. Shall we leave the girls to it.

Patsy and Humphrey exit.

Saffron Mum, what was Patsy?

Edina Oh, darling, it was only for a year and then it fell off.

Saffron Mum, I think I'm going to be sick. Help me.

Edina slides under the table.

scene ten Exterior villa by the swimming pool. Day three.

Camera pans across the roof-tops of Marrakech with its tall minarets, the sound of calling to prayer, then pans down to Edina and Patsy lounging by the pool half naked and drinking gin and tonics.

Edina Oh how are you feeling, all right? Are you all right?

Patsy Yeah, I'm feeling good.

Edina Have you seen Saffy this . . .

Patsy Little toad.

Edina I don't think we need worry, darling. I don't think she'll remember anything about last night. Oh sh . . ., sh . . . Here she comes.

Saffron appears with towel wrapped around her.

Edina (*To Saffron.*) Did you find any swimsuits?

Saffron Haven't you got any low-cut ones?

Edina We haven't any knee-length swimsuits, darling, with us.

Saffron (*Worried about sunburn.*) Have you got cream on, Mum?

Edina Olive oil . . .

Saffron I think I might have a swim first.

Edina All right, sweetie. C'mon, c'mon take this off . . . (*Making a grab at the towel.*) No one's looking at you, darling.

Saffron goes for a swim. Edina and Patsy look at her closely. She then climbs out of the pool.

Patsy Quite big tits.

Saffron (*Embarrassed.*) Mum!

Edina You should have waxed, darling. That dilapadatory cream's no good at all.

Saffron I thought we were going to look around. You can't just sit by the pool all day, you could be anywhere.

Patsy I'm not moving.

Edina Darling, we just need to be recharged by luxury after our journey.

Patsy You deserve it.

Saffron Well, what about the shopping you wanted to get in?

Patsy Shopping?

Edina Shopping? (*Suddenly interested.*) We should . . . We should go shopping.

Patsy Oh, I think so.

Edina Before we know it, they'll have found the bloody equipment and we'll have to do some work or something.

scene eleven Marrakech Street Market.

Edina, Patsy and Saffron are mingling with the crowds. Heads are turning –
Edina is attracting attention. She is only half-dressed.

Saffron I wish you'd cover yourself up, Mum.

Edina Look, darling, these people don't mind. Now, I've got to get some jewellery boxes . . . boxes, bowls, plates, rugs, djalabas . . . What about you, Pats?

Patsy I'm just gonna get some little gorgeous things.

Saffron We should have got a guide.

Edina Oh, stop it. I know this place, darling. I know these people. (*Tries a bit of fake Moroccan.*) La car car car eh su. (*An old man spits at her.*)

Edina Don't start buying anything yet. We're not in the proper souk here. What are they all looking at? What are they all looking at? What are they all looking at?

Saffron They're looking at you.

Edina Well, I know they're looking at me, darling. I don't particularly care about that. You're never gonna see any of these people ever again in your whole life.

Saffron You're asking for trouble.

Edina (*To gaping passersby.*) Stare – Hallo! Hallo! Hallo! Stare. Stare.

Edina (*Indicating carpet.*) Well, you see that's quite nice, isn't it. But I mean, that's two-a-penny in Liberty's basement.

They move on.

Saffron That's nice, Mum . . .

Edina What I want is one of those sort of, you know, kaftan sort of things that the women wear.

Edina (*Moving on to next stall.*) This is a pile of crap. (*They move on.*) It didn't used to be like this down here. It's so touristy now, isn't it.

Patsy I know, it's changed rather a lot.

Edina It used to be so chic.

Saffron (*Giving sudden squeal.*) Oh! Mum, that man just pinched me!

Patsy Don't worry. He's obviously very old and completely blind.

Saffron Thanks very much.

Edina Well, no one's pinched me. No one's pinched me yet.

They move on.

Edina (*To street-seller.*) No, I don't want the bracelets, darling. You can get those two-a-penny in Liberty's. (*A local puts a hawk on Edina's arm.*) Sweetie, darling, someone's put an insect on me!

They move on.

Edina I'm starving now.

Saffron Do you know what starving means?

Edina All right, I'm hungry – I'm starving. All right, I'm starving.

Saffron Stop moaning.

Edina Let's go to a hotel, darling, and get a drink, sweetie? They don't have any bars or anything. No bars.

Patsy disappears into a shop.

Saffron Where's Patsy?

Edina She's in the stall with all those dried-up things.

Saffron Oh . . . She should feel at home then.

Edina (*To Patsy, as she rejoins them with a substance around her nose.*) Sweetie. Shall we go to the hotel and get a nice drink? A little gin?

Patsy Yeah, that'd be nice.

They move on.

Saffron (*Indicating food.*) If you're starving you'd eat this.

They stop at a local food stall where pots of meat are boiling away.

Edina (*Looking in pot.*) Sweetie. If they took the face off, I'd eat it.

It is now clear they are lost.

Edina (*Walking on.*) I know where it is. Look, darling, we go through a couple of these stalls here. Just here through this thing here. Just here, darling. Just here, darling.

Saffron Are you sure?

Edina Well . . . I don't know, do I? You just wanna hold your nose, darling. Meat. (*Pointing.*) Oh, it's over there, darling. (*To Patsy.*) Can you see, sweetie. Can you see?

They set off. Camera pulls back to reveal that they are trying to walk through the 'square where all humanity meets'. There are thousands of people.

Saffron (*Interrupting.*) Mum, people keep taking things . . .

Edina (*To Patsy.*) Now, darling, we're only over there. Over there.

Patsy (*Struggling to see.*) I would, Eddy. If I could see where I was going. Instead of forever just trailing behind this little insect.

Edina Oh, come on. Stop bloody moaning.

Saffron Shut up!

They eventually come out of the crowd the other side. Saffy is not with them.

Edina Oh! Oh! Where's Saff? What have we done with Saff? Where's Saff? Saff? Saff?

Patsy (*Showing her the money. She has sold Saffy.*) Eddy, Eddy. A couple of thousand . . .

Edina (*Pleased.*) She'll be all right.

scene twelve **Interior villa. Day three. Evening.**

Patsy and Edina enter. They are worn out and filthy.

Edina The filth, the stench, the heat . . . I mean, that's the last time I ever step foot into that toilet bowl of Northern Africa. I mean, how dare they spit at me? The nation has a pillowcase with a slit in it as a national costume.

Patsy Eddy – we're here with clean things, clear air, lovely peace and quiet. Lovely gin and tonic.

Edina Yeah. I know. I just, I just don't feel somehow . . . I just don't feel we should've sold Saffy just like that.

Patsy What do you mean like that? It wasn't just like that . . . I had to haggle them up. I got a good exchange rate.

Edina What did you get?

Patsy Well, one sour-faced little ditch-rat for 2,000 dirham, and, darling, she said she wanted to see how the real people lived.

Edina I don't think the white-slave trade was quite what she had in mind.

Patsy Oh, she'll be all right, Eddy.

70
71

Edina She'll be all right, won't she. I mean, it's not as if she enjoyed a normal life anyway, is it?

Patsy No, I mean, it might bring something out in her.

Edina She might just live in painful servitude for the rest of her life.

Patsy Well, I mean, nothing is certain, not for any of us. (*Raising her glass.*) Cheers, Eddy!

Edina Cheers.

scene thirteen Exterior villa. By the pool. Day four.

Patsy and Edina are reading magazines and drinking by the pool. Edina is wearing Pop-Specs. A servant appears with a telephone on a tray.

Manservant Phone, madame.

Patsy . . . moiselle. Mademoiselle – I'll overlook it this time. (*Casting lascivious glances at him.*) (*Speaking on telephone.*) Patsy Stone. Yeah. Oh, no, are you sure? (*Hangs up.*) Damn, damn, damn, damn, damn.

Edina Bit of bad news, darling?

Patsy Yeah, it appears the equipment's turned up. They want to shoot this afternoon. I've got to meet them by this . . . wall.

Edina I don't have to come, do I?

Patsy If you want your crappo specs to appear in high-class glossy print. (*She groans, holding stomach.*)

Edina Oh, are you all right, darling? Have you eaten something?

Patsy No. Not since 1973.

scene fourteen **By the wall. In the Atlas Mountains.**

Edina and Patsy are standing with Ali who has driven them there. It is a rural village and there are children playing around.

Patsy This is the wall. I recognize this bit from the photograph.

Ali I have to go to see some other people. *Vogue* are shooting further up in the mountains.

Patsy *Vogue*?

Ali And I have to go to arrange catering for a movie that is shooting here, too. (*He brings the huge case of shoot clothes and leaves it by Patsy.*)

Edina Oh! What movie?

Ali It's the *Life of Christ II*.

Edina Who is Jesus these days?

Ali Err . . . Charles Dance. I'll come back and check you're okay later.

Patsy Er, no, no. Go away and just don't bother to come back. Just go and don't come back.

Ali leaves in the car.

Edina Are you sure?

Patsy He's working for *Vogue*, Eddy. We don't want him around.

Edina Oh!

Edina (*Looking around at the children.*) Have you seen the way all these children are dressed, darling. I mean, why is it the hottest countries in the world, they put them all in these old woolly jumpers. You'd think Gap would've spotted the hole in the market, wouldn't you. I mean, a whole population here just crying out for good-quality reasonably priced kids' casuals.

Patsy Oh, shut up Eddy.

They wait.

Edina I don't think they're coming, Pats.

Patsy I need a loo.

They continue to wait.

scene fifteen By the same wall. Later still.

They are still waiting. The children have gone.

Edina What are we going to do?

Patsy Oh, bastards! Eddy, I really need to go to the loo now. Let's just go and find a hotel or café or somethin' and you can phone, and I will go to the loo. There must be a centre of town somewhere out here.

Edina I'll order some champagne, darling.

scene sixteen

Edina and Patsy are staggering along dusty road pulling the huge suitcase. The road seems to go on for ever. They start to head across country which is a big mistake. Patsy is still dying to go to the loo.

Edina I mean, the gutter's all right for you in London, isn't it? I mean, you go in the gutter and rush hour traffic in front of a whole party of your friends . . . But no, you're not going to dig a hole and just go here now. Um? (*Pointing.*) Look, somewhere over there . . .

A boy passes on a donkey. Patsy, carrying the suitcase on her back, falls into a ditch. They are now in the middle of nowhere.

Edina Oh, God, streuth. I mean, this place is enough to make you want to call Sting.

Patsy (*Delving into the suitcase.*) Well, look, we'll just take what we need and we can just dump the suitcase.

Edina For God's sake, we'll be eating each other within an hour . . . We're not gonna worry about the luggage.

Patsy Well, which way do we go?

Edina Well, I don't know. Let's just follow the donkey, darling. It must be going somewhere.

scene seventeen Market with donkey park.

Edina and Patsy walk through the donkey park, reeling at the sights and smells.

Edina I think I'm going to faint. What is that smell?

Patsy I think it's fish.

scene eighteen By river.

Camera pans over an almost deserted town. From a distance Patsy and Edina approach. Patsy is seated on a donkey. The Pop-Specs bag is tucked inside her clothes, giving the impression that she is pregnant. Edina is walking ahead, leading the donkey.

74

75

Edina (*Feet hurting.*) Ow . . .

Patsy What's the matter now, darling?

Edina Well, it's my turn on the donkey now. You said by the time we got here it would be my turn.

Patsy Well, I'm not moving. Ow . . . ow.

Edina What's the matter with you, anyway?

Patsy Just don't question me.

Edina (*Exhausted.*) Oh, God.

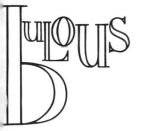

scene nineteen Village. Light fading.

Patsy (*Spotting a house.*) Look, hang on . . . Look over there.

Edina (*Approaching the house.*) Oh . . . Oh, God. There's no bell. (*A window opens. A face peers out.*) Hallo? Hallo? Have you got a toilette pour . . . (*Window closes.*) . . . a madame?

Patsy Mademoiselle.

Edina Look, can't you just go in a hole somewhere, darling?

They move on, then stop at another house.

Patsy Go on, Eddy, over there. Come on.

Edina Let me do the talking, sweetie, for this. (*An old man comes out.*) Hotel?

The man beckons them to follow, and leads them to a horrible stable.

Patsy Oh, he's got a hotel.

Edina He could be a mass-murderer for all we know.

The man points at the stable and walks off.

Edina (*To man.*) Here? Here? Are you kidding?

Edina and Patsy are repelled, but Patsy is determined to enter.

Patsy Oh, well it looks fine actually.

Edina No, I can't stay here.

Patsy Look, Eds, it's lovely. Just let me in here. Let me in.

Edina No! No!

scene twenty Exterior stable. Day five.

Edina a Patsy emerge looking really rough. They are still clutching the Pop-Specs and a Polaroid camera. Edina starts taking polaroids.

Edina You never know ... Conran might want that, darling.

Patsy The bloody donkey's gone.

Edina Shit! It was my turn on the bloody donkey!

They set off walking.

scene twenty-one Moroccan street.

Edina and Patsy pass a little figure in a yashmak. The figure stops and looks at them. They are so used to being stared at, they walk wearily on.

Saffron Mum!

Edina and Patsy turn. The figure takes off the headdress—it is Saffy.

Patsy Damn!

Edina (*Embarrassed.*) Oh, darling, sweetie. (*Goes to Saffy and hugs her.*)

Saffron Where did you go?

Edina We've found you, darling!

Edina Pats ... It's ...

Patsy Fantastic.

scene twenty-two Interior villa. Day five.

All, plus Humphrey, are sitting around having food and drink.

Humphrey Well, what bad luck! Ha-ha-ha.

Saffy glares at Patsy.

Patsy (*To Saffron.*) It was a joke. I didn't think anyone would be idiot enough to take you.

Edina (*Covered in bites and sunburn.*) Not much of a holiday it's been so far, is it, eh?

Patsy It wasn't a holiday, Eddy.

Edina All right, not a holiday. Not a holiday. We haven't got any Pop-Specs' photos, any merchandising, any of the shopping. The only thing I was in danger of sleeping with was a donkey and even he did a runner!

Humphrey But you must have a good time in your few final days. You must see the real Marrakech. (*Picking up brochure.*) 'Everything from sabre-wielding horsemen to the Elizabeth Taylor Kaftan Museum'.

As Humphrey continues to read from the brochure, Edina is embarrassing Saffy by winking suggestively and making sexy gestures.

Humphrey I quote this, you know, from the brochure. 'Marrakech has an elusive character all of its own. Wickedly grinning old men ready to paddle for hour after hour . . .' Oh, there'll be no end of treats in store. You'll be treated like film stars. Like Ava Gardner and um . . . companion. (*To Yentob.*) Ah – Yentob (*Snaps his fingers to indicate hubble-bubbles.*) (*To his guests.*) Now enjoy, enjoy. (*Yentob brings in the hubble-bubbles.*) I have to go see a camel about a hump.

Edina This is heaven, darling . . .

Patsy Fantastic!

Edina Get plugged in, Saffy. Come on. Get plugged in.

Credits.

scene twenty-three Interior villa. Three days later. Morning.

Saffy is packed, ready to leave. Edina and Patsy are comatose on the sofas.

Saffron Come on . . . Wake up . . .

Edina and Patsy stir reluctantly.

Edina Oh, God, did I fall asleep here? Oh damn. Wake up, Pats. Wake up, darling. Oh, catch up on a bit of luxury, sweetie. Well, I'm going to have some breakfast and then sit by the pool or something.

Saffron We've got to go. It's Friday.

Patsy Friday!

Saffron You've been unconscious for three days.

Edina/Patsy No!

Saffy leans over Edina to get her coat from the back of the sofa.

Edina (*Sniffing Saffy's body.*) What's that smell? What's that smell? Is that you, sweetie? That sort of honey, yoghurty smell? Is that you?

Saffron flees, overcome with embarrassment. Yentob winks.

ABSOLUTELY ffa

new best friends

Cast List

Edina · JENNIFER SAUNDERS
Patsy · JOANNA LUMLEY
Saffron · JULIA SAWALHA
Mother · JUNE WHITFIELD
Bubble · JANE HORROCKS
Catriona · HELEN LEDERER
Fleur · HARRIET THORPE
Hamish · ADRIAN EDMONDSON
Carmen · JO BRAND
Suzy · MEERA SYAL
Bettina · MIRANDA RICHARDSON
Max · PATRICK BARLOW
As herself · ZANDRA RHODES
As herself · LULU
As herself · BRITT

FABULOUS

scene one Edina's kitchen. Day one. Morning.

Edina comes down the stairs, late as usual, expecting Saffy to be there. She is hung over.

Edina Oh, sweetie. I'm not going in to the office today because Bettina and Max are coming and I've got to clear the whole house up for them, darling. Anyway, did I tell you, Bubble's not there any more. She's gone. I mean, someone offered her a pathetic junior post at *Marie Claire* so I accepted for her. Let them pay her, darling, while we've got no work on. (*Notices that she has been talking to herself and is confused. Saffy is always there, but not this morning. There is only the sound of distant hoovering. She is frightened.*) Oh! Sweetie? Darling? Oh, God . . . Oh, God . . .(*She is now very frightened and begins to move slowly about the kitchen frightening herself even more. She moves to the window, and looks out. There is the sharp clicking sound of someone wearing high heels walking past along the pavement outside. She waits expectantly, but they pass by. A fly is buzzing on the window in front of her. She leans forward to get a closer look when a voice from behind startles her and she screams.*)

Saffron Mum? What are you doing? What's the matter?

Edina Don't ever do that again, darling. Don't you ever just go and leave me on my own like that.

Saffron I was upstairs. What were you looking at?

Edina (*Embarrassed.*) Nothing, sweetie.

Saffron Nothing? You were checking the fly, weren't you?

Edina I have to, darling.

Saffron I didn't think you still did that. It's been ten years since you saw that film and Jeff Goldblum is now full-sized, wingless and living happily ever after in LA.

Edina I know that, darling, but you'll be laughing the other side of your face the day you squash something with a little tiny human head against that window, darling, as it screams 'No, no, I'm a professor of physics, take me back to my laboratory'. You'll wish you were a Buddhist then, darling.

Saffron What drugs were you taking last night?

Edina Patsy had them, not me.

Saffron What?

Edina I said Patsy had them. What are you looking at? Why's it always my fault? Patsy had them . . . Patsy had the Ecstas . . . Ecstasy, sweetie. I just said no. No to drugs. No-no-no.

Saffron Well, something kept you going till three o'clock this morning.

Edina Just a little coke, sweetie.

Saffron Mum, as you've got Bettina and Max coming to stay and I've got a lot of work to do in the next few days, I thought I might move into the Halls of Residence.

Edina Oh, oh well, you're just going to leave me, are you? You're just going to go? You're not going to stay around and help me, darling. You're just going to go. Oh, well, all right then. Just go, go – go on.

Saffron There's plenty of food in, and the bedroom is clean.

Edina Oh bugger, bugger, bugger, buggery-bollocks, darling.

Saffron What?

Edina Well, darling. I was going to totally refurnish the spare room. You don't seem to realize, darling. Bettina and Max are coming.

Saffron So?

Edina Bettina, darling, the Queen of Minimalism, darling. I mean, look, look . . . how I am dressed today . . . Minimalist, darling. I mean, she's coming here to London, to this, darling. (*She becomes obsessed with tidying in an effort to be Minimalist.*) She's gonna think this is what I think is so great. Objets central, this . . . you . . . All this clutter, darling.

Saffron Well, tidy it up then if you don't like it.

Edina I will. I just want surfaces, darling. (*Flinging herself around the* *kitchen, picking up and putting down objects.*) Where have all my surfaces gone? Uh? I just want clean lines and surfaces. I don't want this, darling. Look. (*Lifts cup from surface.*) I don't want things on places like that. Things on places. Look . . . I don't want that. (*Holding up a pencil.*) Is this yours?

Saffron Yes.

Edina Could it not be left around. Does it not have a home to go to?

Mother (*Entering.*) That could have been you talking then, Saffy.

Edina Oh, God. What do you want? I've got enough trouble with surplus furniture without occasional old people scattered around the place.

Mother Have you seen my *Take a Break*, dear? I left it here last night.

Edina For someone else to pick up, did you, yeah?

Saffron It's over there, Gran.

Mother Oh, thank you.

She goes and gets it, takes it to the table, and sits down to read it. Edina straightens the magazine to make it look tidy. She then notices Saffron is peeling an orange.

Edina (*To Saffron.*) Come on! Eat it, clear it, eat it, clear it.

Saffron Stop it! Let me finish and then I'll help you. Don't get in such a state.

The buzzer sounds.

Edina Oh! Oh! Now who's that? Someone else to fill the house up.

Mother Now, here we are. How to win a lifetime's supply of tough Melamine stylish garden furniture . . .

Saffron But you haven't got a garden, Gran.

Mother Well, no, but they don't know that, dear.

Patsy (*Entering.*) Morning, Eddy.

ABSOLUTELY fa

She puts her bag down, Edina picks it up and puts it neatly on Patsy's lap.

Edina Morning, darling. (*She looks at Mother.*) Uh! You're gonna have to go. Come on – you're gonna have to go. C'mon ... out you go. C'mon.

Mother But, dear, I've just ...

Edina Come on, just close your sad-rag and clear. Come on.

Patsy starts to light a fag. Edina takes the match and puts an ashtray in her hand. Patsy is confused.

Patsy Are we having lunch, Eds?

Edina No, I'm too busy. (*To Mother.*) Come on close, close, close ...

Mother closes magazine very slowly, gets up and starts to leave.

Saffron Bettina and Max are coming to stay for a few days.

Mother Oh, Bettina. How is she? (*To Edina.*) You two used to get on so well ... Didn't they, Patsy?

Patsy Did they?

Mother Oh, yes. And I encouraged it, dear. Far more suitable than poor, dear, sad, old Patsy. She was such a neat girl.

Patsy Neat? She was so anally retentive she couldn't sit down for fear of sucking up the furniture.

scene two Flashback late 60s. Interior Bettina's house.

Inside the room is stark white. A pure white box. On one wall there is a piece of art, a geometric collage. Hanging in the middle of the room is a metal sculpture, a huge chrome wind chime hanging a couple of feet above the floor. Four white plastic chairs have been arranged in one corner of the room. That is all. Bettina is dressed in a foil dress. Her hair has been pulled strictly back. She is wearing thick black-rimmed spectacles, as is Max who is dressed all in white. Edina and Patsy enter.

Edina Hi! This is great.

Bettina We like it. We think it's the new millennium.

Max (*Coming to greet Edina and Patsy.*) We're really comfortable here ... We feel it's progressive.

Edina I bought you this.

She hands them a bottle of red wine. Bettina takes it and hands it to Max. Neither knows what to do with it. They try putting it down in various places, but it upsets them. Max eventually leaves it outside the door.

Bettina (*To Edina.*) I want to show you my new collection of jewellery. I took inspiration from the new Electrographic architecture. Come and sit down. Max have you seen it? It's in a white box somewhere.

Max (*Looking around brilliant white interior.*) White box ...?

Edina looks at Patsy who is bored stiff. They move over to the chairs. Camera follows Bettina, Edina and Max. Suddenly there is a loud clanging. Patsy has walked into the metal sculpture and is entangled. The noise is deafening. Max and Bettina are frantic, and Edina embarrassed.

Patsy (*Hurt.*) Aaargh!

Edina (*Panicking.*) Damn you, Patsy! You shouldn't have come, you know. You shouldn't have come!

Flashback fades.

scene three Edina's kitchen. Day one. As before.

Edina is nervously tidying up, emptying Patsy's ashtray.

Patsy (*Referring to the metal sculpture.*) I should have sued. I was cut to ribbons, scarred for life.

Saffron (*Indicating facelift scars.*) Extraordinary how it managed to hit you in exactly the same place behind each ear?

Edina Sweetie ...!

Patsy Go on, Eddy . . . Go on, go on.

Edina What?

Patsy Well, go on, go on. You were going to tell this little trail of cat-sick that I was badly injured and not to question me.

Edina No, I wasn't, darling. I was going to say sweetie, darling, if you want to be some help to Mamma you can go upstairs and clear surfaces. (*Indicating Mother.*) Take her with you . . . Take her with you. Clear her . . . Clear her. (*To Patsy.*) Well, you could go too, you know, darling.

Saffy and Mother exit.

Patsy (*Starting to sulk.*) Well, then . . . What, no lunch then, Eds?

Edina Oh, not unless Bettina arrives early in which case I shall have lunch with her.

Patsy Can I borrow the car?

Edina No, it's picking Bettina up from the airport.

Patsy is now in full sulk, standing with head bowed like a small child.

Edina Oh, God, oh God. What's the matter?

Patsy I'm not happy.

Edina Well, take the car. Just go – go.

Patsy I don't want the car.

Edina Well, just go and be unhappy somewhere else. Go on.

Patsy mutters incoherently.

Edina Go. Go on. (*Patsy does not move.*) Bugger off!

Edina touches Patsy's arm to move her. Patsy twitches her arm away. There is a very bad atmosphere, and Patsy mutters something horrible under her breath.

Patsy Don't touch me . . .

Edina Just bugger off! (*Yelling.*) Saff! Saff!

86
87

Patsy flicks ash all over the table, stubs fag out on floor, knocks the ashtray off and storms out, sweeping objects off staircase ledge.

scene four Interior magazine office. Day one.

Open-plan layout for all the departments, but a little separate office for Magda, which has a glass front so can be seen into from the main part. There are ten people working, including Fleur and Catriona sitting amongst a pile of free make-up samples and products. Bubble is there in Magda's office doing nothing. Hamish is sitting eating. Suzy, the art director, is working on the new cover. There are motorbike couriers coming and going and rails of clothes being taken in and out. Fleur and Catriona are trying out various make-up samples.

Catriona Did you go to the Spas last week?

Fleur In Florida? Yes, I did the Fasting Cure.

Catriona Oh! Cure . . . Is it to cure you of fasting or something?

Fleur It does do that, of course, but really it's to lose weight.

Catriona Oh, that sounds good. Is it expensive?

Fleur How do you mean?

Catriona Oh, well, does it cost a lot?

Fleur Absolutely nothing.

Carmen (*Enters, carrying airline food tray, and sits down at her desk. She is pissed off with travelling.*) It's taken all bloody day to do a journey that takes a couple of hours. How many bastards need to look at my ticket and then stare inexplicably at a crap computer screen for hours on end? What is the point of asking me if I packed my bag myself? 'Oh, no, I let some total bastard of Middle Eastern origins pack it for me.'

Patsy enters. They all look at her amazed. She never comes into the office.

Patsy Where's Magda?

Suzy Er ... Is there a meeting or something? Because I'm not ready. I mean, nobody seems to realize how difficult my job is. I mean, I've got the cover photo obviously, but I haven't fitted the words on yet. I mean everybody seems to think that my job just happens ...

Patsy Suzy – I just want to know if she wants lunch.

Suzy Oh! (*She relaxes and goes back to her computer, where her assistant is just getting up from the keyboard.*) Is it my turn yet, Hani? (*She sits and begins to play a computer game.*) Oh, did you get to the Castledrome on level three?

Patsy (*Looks into the office and sees Bubble swinging around in Magda's chair.*) What's she doing there?

Fleur Mags nabbed her from *Marie Claire*.

Patsy enters the office. Bubble is spinning at quite a speed now in the chair.

Patsy Does Eddy know you're here?

Bubble stops spinning and flies off the chair. Has difficulty standing.

Bubble Oh! What?

Patsy Where's Mags' diary? I want to know what she's doing for lunch.

Bubble She's got a meeting.

Patsy (*Looking in the diary.*) Well, why haven't you written it in?

Bubble I'm not completely useless you know. (*Tapping her head.*) It's all in here. It's with someone called ... No, it's gone.

Patsy I'll wait for her.

Bubble Well, shall I get someone to look after you?

Patsy I work here.

Bubble Snap!

Carmen I threw up the Business Class crap over the Pyrenees ... (*Holds up airline food tray.*) But I managed to nick this off a kiddie in Economy on my way back from the toilet.

Hamish Where have you been?

Carmen Spain.

Hamish Ah, off the beaten track . . . Andalusia, forgotten Catalania. My own secret Majorca.

Carmen More like my own secret arsehole. It was a shitty bit of coastline ruined by patronizing English gits. (*Imitating voice.*) 'Oh you must come over and share a rather fine local Rioja. Oh, piss off you sad twats!' (*Blows a raspberry and switches on her word processor as Hamish comes and stands by her.*)

Hamish Oh, dear. Mr Dictionary seems to have deserted us again.

scene five Interior Edina's hallway. Day one.

The house has been cleared of any ornamentation. Saffy is coming down the stairs carrying a bag. Edina rushes up from the kitchen dressed beautifully simply.

Edina (*To Saffron.*) Bettina and Max! Clear! Clear! Clear! Clear!

Saffron I'll just say 'Hallo' and then I'll go.

Edina No-no-no! You're not gonna just say hallo. You just get back here, stand flat against the wall, just hold your bag close, darling. When they come, you go. (*She goes to the door and opens it.*)

Bettina/Max Hi.

They are not quite as Edina expected. Bettina is in her late thirties. Max in his early forties. The baby, which they made a rational decision to have, but were totally unprepared for the reality of, is about three months old. Bettina enters, wearing something crumpled. She has the baby on her shoulder, and cloths and bottles in her hand. She looks absolutely fraught all the time. Max enters behind her. He is dressed casually in jacket, denim shirt, jeans and espadrilles. He looks more relaxed than Bettina, and this is a constant source of annoyance to her. With Max comes a mountain of back-up baby equipment which they always take everywhere. There are changing bags, nappies, bottles, bottle-warmers, packets of dried milk, clothes, blankets, carriers of every

Top The new millennium.

Above The new editor of *Vogue*.

Left 'Very, very, very tired mummy.'

Above Chasing Britt and Lulu.

Right 'My new best friend, Lulu.'

Opposite 'Somebody operate her!'

Above Patsy inhales the kitchen.

Right The cure.

Opposite Court gear.

Top 'Let the swamp blood
flow forth.'

Above 'She didn't take the
rubber gloves off for the
first twelve years.'

Right 'Dull, soulless dance
music.'

Above A Jane Seymour
fantasy birth.

Right 'Is the lady from the
adoption agency here?'

description, pushchair, baskets, collapsible playpen, toys, etc. They have everything the baby might need for the next two years.

Edina Bettina . . . Max . . . Come in. (*She waves at Saffy to leave, and Saffy exits.*)

Bettina Hi.

Max Hi.

Bettina (*To Max.*) Max, can you bring me the other cloth?

Max (*He is slowly bringing the equipment into the hallway.*) Where is the other cloth?

Bettina Er . . . blue bag. Not the terry one . . . You know, the one that was near the bottle-warmer, by the playpen.

Max What the bag that fits the buggy or the backpack?

Bettina No, you know, the one that's . . . er . . . by the mat with the music centre. That one. Same material as the sling.

Max You used it on the plane.

Bettina Oh, no, I didn't. Christ, Max, we only had those four bags and the Moses basket on the plane.

Bettina (*Indicating the baby.*) Is he awake? He's moving.

Max What?

Bettina Well, you can see his face. What's he doing?

Max He's just . . . He's just moving?

Edina (*Indicating baby.*) Do you want to put that down, darling, somewhere?

Bettina Oh, no, he won't go down now. Max can take him in a minute.

Max You could just put him down on the . . .

Bettina No, he won't go down now.

Max Just let me take him!

Bettina Yes, thank you, that would be nice. He isn't exactly light and I have had him since Heathrow and I don't expect to be on my last legs before you offer.

Max Right.

Bettina (*Handing him the baby.*) Now, hand, bottom and head.

Max I've got him, I've got him. Yes.

Edina (*To Bettina.*) Darling, darling, actually do you want ... Do you want a drink, sweetie? Okay, darling? Well, I'll crack open some Bolly.

Max That's a good idea. What? (*In response to Bettina's glare.*) Look, I'm not intending to get drunk.

Bettina Yes, well, that of course is up to you. But how are you going to feel if you drop him or something happens and you know you had that drink?

Max I don't know why we don't do what Jocasta suggested and keep him awake, then he might sleep tonight.

Bettina Oh, Dr bloody-Spock-Casta.

They exit to kitchen.

scene six Interior magazine office. Day one. As before.

Nobody is really doing anything useful. Carmen is tapping away at her word processor. Hamish is watching her. Catriona and Fleur are thinking, and watching Patsy who is looking impatient and pretending that she has something to do. Bubble is spinning on the chair. Suzy is at her computer.

Hamish (*To Carmen.*) Listen, you old tart. Can we not think of a nice way of putting this? How about 'We grazed on canapés and feasted on roasted suckling pig and juicy carciofi beneath a bewildering array of stars beside a pool brimming with azure blue . . .' You can't put 'We all sat around and ate free foreign crap then vomited'.

Carmen (*Amazed.*) But I'm a journalist.

Hamish Fair enough.

The telephone rings.

Suzy Hani, darling. Would you get that? Get that Hani! I can't . . . (*Phone still ringing.*) Somebody get it . . . (*She is tapping away maniacally at the computer.*) . . . Damn . . . Damn . . . (*Gives up and answers the phone.*) Yeah, oh, all right, yeah, I'll tell them. (*Puts phone down and says to Bubble.*) Mags is out for lunch. Damn!

Bubble (*Stops spinning.*) Oh, right.

Patsy Damn!

Bubble (*To Patsy.*) Aaaaaaaah? (*Swaying.*) What are you going to do?

Patsy I'll ring up an old friend or . . .

Bubble An *old* friend? Old? Meeting your old friend?

Patsy Shut up. I'm meeting a very, very-very dear-dear-dear-dear old friend.

Bubble Well, don't forget your Zimmer frame.

Patsy exits.

scene seven Interior Edina's kitchen. Day one.

There are bits of baby equipment on every surface. Bettina, fag in mouth, is scrubbing out and sterilizing baby bottles. Edina is sitting at the table, watching her.

Bettina It was a Caesarean in the end, because of complications. Nothing to do with my age. So, of course, I felt butchered for a couple of months, but I lost the weight almost immediately, which, of course, doesn't happen if you have them younger. (*Looking Edina up and down.*) I mean, you've never lost it, have you? You seem to get away with it somehow, despite your criminal dress sense. (*Holding up dirty nappies.*) Got somewhere I can put these?

Edina Chuck 'em on the floor.

Bettina You know, we've tried to be green, but it's just not humanly possible.

Max's voice comes through a baby intercom that is attached to Bettina's waist like a walkie-talkie. There is a lot of rustling noise as well, and it is difficult to hear what he is saying.

Max (Voice Over) Have you got it on?

Bettina (*Speaking into the intercom.*) Can you hear me? If you talk that loudly you're going to wake him.

Max (Voice Over) He's in the sitting-room. I'll check that one now.

Bettina (*To Edina.*) Oh, God! Do you still see anything of that old alcoholic?

Edina What Patsy? Oh, just off and on. You know, darling.

Max (Voice Over) I'm in the ... Oh ...

The baby begins to cry over the intercom.

Bettina Oh shit, shit, shit. (*There is the sound of a mobile being wound up and music begins to play. The baby stops crying.*).

Bettina He should just bring him down because he'll never go back now. (*Speaking into the intercom.*) Just ... just bring him down. Bring him down now.

Max enters with the baby and Bettina fusses around. The baby has gone back to sleep. Edina is bored.

Bettina (*To Max.*) Just sit! Sit! (*He reaches for bottles of champagne.*) Leave it!

Max (*Trying to organize the baby's feed.*) SMA! SMA! Okay.

Bettina Yes, kettle, kettle ...

ABSOLUTELY fa

Max Spoon, knife, knife, bottle, bottle, bottle, top, teat, bottle.

Edina (*More than ready to escape.*) I'm going to see Patsy. I'll see you later, darling.

She exits.

Max (*To Bettina.*) Get me the knife . . . knife . . .

Bettina (*Searching frantically.*) Knife, knife, kettle, kettle, kettle . . .

Bettina His eyes are open. Quick . . . get the flash cards. Where are they? We had them on the plane . . .

Max indicates they are in his back pocket, and Bettina takes them out.

Max Say the words as well.

Bettina (*Holds up card.*) Yes, yes, mummy . . . mummy . . . mummy. (*Exhausted.*) Very, very tired mummy.

scene eight Interior magazine office. Day one.

The office is empty apart from Suzy who is working on the magazine cover. Edina enters looking for Patsy to have lunch. Suzy hears footsteps and leaps into action. She rushes to the computer and starts to play.

Suzy (*Realizing she has made a mistake.*) Oh, I was working! I don't know why I did that. Actually, I was over here working. No, you, you don't understand. I was actually . . .

Edina (*To Bubble.*) Are you still here?

Bubble Just . . .

Edina Well, have you seen Pats?

Bubble Yeah, but she's not here.

Edina Where is she?

Bubble She's . . .

Suzy At lunch . . .

Bubble (*Remembering.*) Oh, that's right, with a very old-old-old-old-old-old-old-old-old-old friend.

Edina (*Disappointed.*) Oh, damn. Well, you can go back to the office now. We've got some work on.

Bubble No, I can't.

Edina Why not?

Bubble I've been head-shrunk.

Suzy Hunted.

Bubble Head-hunted. Head-hunted by *Vogue*. Is that a magazine or something?

Edina That's a magazine. By *Vogue*, darling? You've been head-hunted? As what?

Bubble (*Trying to remember.*) Er . . . Editor. (*Closes Edina's mouth.*) See thee. (*Exits.*)

Edina Damn!

`scene nine` London traffic.

Driving along in her car, Edina spots Patsy window-shopping outside Betsy Jackson. They pretend not to see each other, and Patsy rushes into the shop waving her arm and pretending she has seen a friend. Edina drives on to the Conran shop, passes through it, and continues to Joseph's. She emerges a few minutes later carrying several bags, and continues on her way to Joe's Café.

`scene ten` Interior Joe's Café.

Edina, trying to look laid-back, is sitting fiddling with her cigarettes. Patsy enters, but pretends not to see Edina. At that moment, Zandra Rhodes comes in looking for her friend, Britt.

Patsy (*Grabbing Zandra Rhodes.*) Oh, Zandra, hi. It's me . . . Patsy . . . Patsy Stone.

Zandra (*Obviously not recognizing her.*) Hi.

Patsy (*Following her to her table.*) Yes, I will join you. Thank you, darling.

Britt (*Seated at the table.*) Oh, Zandra, hallo.

Zandra (*To Patsy.*) Do you know Britt?

Patsy Oh, hi Britt ... It's Patsy.

Britt (*Nonplussed.*) Patsy?

Patsy Stone.

Britt (*Puzzled. Searching her memory.*) Stone?

Patsy Patsy, Patsy, Stone. Stone. Patsy. Patsy Stone.

Britt (*Faking.*) Oh, Patsy!

Patsy (*Delighted.*) Oh, Britts!

Britt Pats!

Patsy Britt.

Britt Pat.

Patsy Bri ...

Britt Pa ...

Patsy Br ...

Britt P ...

Patsy B ...

Waiter Can I get you a drink, madame?

Patsy ... moiselles. Bottle of red, please.

Britt Er ... no, thank you, I don't drink.

Zandra Just some water, please.

Patsy Well, just the one will do then.

Patsy Oh, look, it's little Lulu. Hi, Lu!

Edina (*Noticing Lulu grabs her.*) Lulu, Lulu, hallo!

Lulu I'm not meeting you, am I?

Edina No, no – Edina, we've met before.

Lulu Yes, I know, but I'm not supposed to be having lunch with you. I would rather be on my table on my own.

Edina No, you wouldn't.

Lulu Let . . . let go of my jacket.

Edina (*Desperately.*) I need to talk to you.

Lulu It's not about one of those benefits or one of those awful parties or something? I haven't forgiven you for the Albert Hall fiasco.

Edina Well, I'm sorry about that one, but it said on the invitation that it would be lovely if you got up and did a few numbers. You know, sing 'Shout' and that sort of thing.

Lulu There wasn't even a band.

Edina It was for charity.

Lulu What do you want?

Edina and Patsy exchange glances. Patsy pretends she is having a wonderful time.

Lulu I'm off.

Edina Listen, I may well have a gun in my bag. I will shoot you and try very hard to turn it on myself if you leave, all right? I'll pay for the meal. All right and the champagne, and a substantial donation to the charity of your choice. All right.

Lulu (*Haggling.*) Three-courses and pudding or I'm walking. And don't talk to me . . . and don't smoke. I'm starving!

Edina Lulu. What would you like, Lulu?

Lulu (*Studies the menu.*) Oh, I'd like one of those.

Edina Um–hum, yes.

Lulu And, er, I'll have two of those.

Edina Yes, Lulu.

Lulu And I'll have three of these.

Edina Steady on, sweetie.

Lulu And . . . er, just get me the champagne, okay?

Edina Champagne for Lulu!

Patsy (*Competing madly.*) Well, this is fantastic, like a reunion.

Britt Er, where did you two first meet?

Zandra I think it was in a make-up shop in Carnaby Street?

Patsy Lady Jaynes. That was the first time I met you, do you remember? I was having my tits painted.

Britt As what?

Zandra To look like tits.

Patsy That's right. Fantastic! And then we two used to work together all the time.

Zandra can't really remember having worked with Patsy back in the 60s.

Zandra I think we did *a* session.

Patsy Zandra, *all* the time – you just wanted my body and your clothes. We just worked and worked and worked.

scene eleven **Photographer's studio. Flashback late 60s. Photo shoot.**

Patsy is a model posing in one of Zandra's creations. Photographer is trying to take some photographs. His assistants are trying to make the dress stand out at the sides with a fishing line. Patsy keeps falling over.

Photographer Look, I need that dress out at the sides. What is she doing?

Patsy falls over.

Zandra (*To Patsy.*) Come on, pull yourself together.

Photographer (*To Zandra.*) I've only got her here because she's your friend.

Zandra I just felt sorry for her. I hardly know her.

scene twelve Interior Joe's Café.

Zandra is just leaving.

Britt I'll come and see you.

Patsy Bye, sweetie, bye, sweetie, sweetie, bye. Bye, Zandra. Bye, sweetie.

Britt Yeah.

Patsy Yeah, the Portobello Road.

Britt The Kings Road.

Patsy The Carnaby . . . Road. Biba, Quant.

Britt Vidal.

Patsy Tiffin and Foale, The Shrimp.

Britt The Twig.

Patsy The Stones, The Beatles, The Marquee . . .

Britt The Small Faces . . .

Patsy Terry and Julie.

Britt Um, Peter and Gordon.

Patsy Jack and . . . Michael.

Britt John . . .

Patsy . . . and Mary.

Britt I don't know you at all, do I?

Patsy No.

Britt leaves her.

Edina (*To waiter.*) Can we have the bill? The bill?

Lulu (*Licking the plate.*) Oh, that was delicious, thanks.

Edina Oh, now she talks, now she talks. I was gonna say, I really enjoyed your last single 'Independence . . .' (*Sings.*)

Lulu I've had two since then.

Edina Have you? I didn't know about that. That's ridiculous. I thought you'd gone quiet. Do you know what you need? You need a really good publicity machine. Who does your PR?

Lulu You do.

Lulu (*Spotting Britt.*) How are you doing? Britt – good to see you! How are you?

Britt (*To Lulu.*) Good to see you, too.

Lulu I just had a great lunch.

They exit together.

Edina Lulu, Lulu, Lulu?

Patsy (*Competing madly.*) Bye, Britt. Bye, sweetie, *ciao.*

scene thirteen Edina's kitchen. Day one. Night.

Edina is sitting at the table plotting how to get rid of Bettina and Max. Saffy comes down the stairs.

Edina Hallo, darling.

Saffron I only came back because you said it was an emergency.

Edina It is an emergency, darling. Look at this, darling. Lacroix – baby spew. Baby spew Lacroix! (*Indicating her shoulder and jewellery.*) Baby spew, darling. It *is* an emergency. They've got to go, darling.

Saffron I thought she was your friend.

Edina She is my friend, darling. But now it's the-baby-this, the-baby-that, darling, I mean . . .

Saffron Nobody's been paying enough attention to you.

Edina No.

Saffron Have you tried talking to her, helping her?

Edina Helping her? Helping her? Where's the fun in that, darling? And look at this ... (*Indicating baby paraphernalia.*) Where have all my surfaces gone, darling? It's like living in a small regional branch of Mother-bloody-care, darling, isn't it! They've got to go, darling, so I can return to some degree of normality.

Saffron Whatever that is.

Edina Yes, whatever that is, darling. But it's not this no-fun bloody baby world, is it?

Mother (*Entering.*) Well, I think I've managed to help poor Bettina a little with the baby. She seems to be making so much fuss. I thought it wise to call the doctor. The baby was making some strange noises.

Bettina and Max enter.

Saffron Is everything all right?

Bettina I think he might be going down with a cold, but he's not sure. But, anyway, he's gone to sleep now in our bed, so Max can sleep on the sofa tonight and I'll take the travel cot.

Max (*To Mother.*) Are you all right?

Mother Oh, yes, I'm so sorry I fainted, but I never was very good with nappies of the brown variety.

Max I think I'll, um, turn in.

Bettina (*Reacting hysterically.*) Go on, then, I don't know how you can, but go on.

Max goes to bed.

Edina Is it actually asleep now, then, the baby thing?

Bettina Yeah, yeah.

Saffron (*To Bettina.*) Well, maybe you should get some sleep while he is ...

Bettina (*Beside herself.*) Oh, Christ. This is the only time I have to myself.

Edina (*To Saffron.*) She's lovely, isn't she, darling. She's lovely, isn't she. Well, you can amuse her. I'm going to bed. Goodnight.

Edina exits. The other three sit awkwardly at the table. Saffy eventually speaks.

Saffron (*Politely.*) Has he got any teeth yet?

Bettina Oh, Jesus. You can talk to me about other things, you know. I mean, I'm not a complete vegetable! Well, I'm sorry if I might seem snappy, but it's just . . .

Saffron (*Reassuringly.*) It's all right.

Mother (*Kindly.*) Having a baby can make one very depressed. (*Pointedly.*) I know.

Saffron But you have got a lovely baby. And you've got Max . . . and he's obviously very fond of you.

Mother And he's very good-looking.

Bettina (*Pleased.*) Really? What, you really think so?

Mother Oh, yes.

Saffron You're just tense . . . You need to unwind and relax.

Bettina Yeah. Yeah – I know, I know. You're right, really. I don't know how he puts up with me actually . . .

We hear noises from the intercom mounted on the wall. It is Edina and Max having sex. There is a lot of heavy breathing and rustling noise.

Max (Voice Over) (*To Edina.*) Oh, come on, lie down.

Edina (Voice Over) (*Nervously.*) What if someone comes up though? What if someone comes?

Max (Voice Over) I don't care if the witch catches us. How do you undo this thing?

Edina (Voice Over) Slow down, Max.

Much huffing and puffing. Bettina is sitting bolt upright. Saffy cannot believe her ears.

Max (Voice Over) Ah, ah, I can't. It's so long since I did it. Ah, ah, aaaagh . . .

Edina (Voice Over) Is that it?

Mother (*To Saffron.*) I say, is that Radio Four, dear?

Credits.

scene fourteen Interior Edina's kitchen. Later the same night.

Saffy is standing staring at Edina.

Edina (*To Saffron.*) I had to, darling. They had to go.

Patsy (*Entering cautiously.*) Hi, sweetie.

Edina (*Relieved.*) Hi, darling.

They kiss. Freeze frame.

Cast List
Edina · JENNIFER SAUNDERS
Patsy · JOANNA LUMLEY
Saffron · JULIA SAWALHA
Bubble · JANE HORROCKS
Mother · JUNE WHITFIELD
Malcolm · MARK WING-DAVEY
Justin · CHRISTOPHER MALCOLM

scene one Interior Edina's bedroom. Day one.

Edina is getting dressed into very 70s' gear and make-up. She is plucking her eyebrows, sticking sequins on her face and glitter on her body. For every item she puts on, one is discarded. Jewellery and clothes are thrown around the room. When she is ready, she turns and the whole amazing outfit is revealed.

Edina (*Admiring herself in the mirror.*) Hallo, 1992!

scene two Interior Edina's kitchen. Day one.

Saffron is there, Mother is also there but at the cooker and not immediately visible. Edina enters.

Edina Sorry I was so long, darling. I had to clear out my wardrobe, get rid of all these horrible revolting, unfashionable clothes that I simply would not wear, darling, because they are not fashion. I've put them on the floor to throw out.

Mother I thought you'd put them on, dear.

Edina What are you doing here?

Mother Oh, just thought I'd make the most of the house while you can still afford to keep it up.

Edina Thank you, and how is it that when I look at you all I see is wear-and-tear, wear-and-tear.

Mother (*Looking at Edina.*) I say, I remember those trousers.

Edina No, you don't.

Mother Still hung on to those? Mind you, I'm surprised you can still get into them. It was rather like trying to get toothpaste back into the tube, even then.

Edina These are new ... Tell her, Saffy darling. The 70s are back.

Mother Oh! Does that mean you'll be voting Labour again, dear?

Edina (*To Saffron.*) I've always voted Labour, sweetie. Anyway, I'm only talking about fashion.

Saffron Thank God for that. I wouldn't want to go through that childhood again.

Edina Oh, darling – make Mummy a cup of coffee, darling. Would you, sweetie, from the new machine, darling?

Mother Oooh, a chappaccino.

Edina (*Spelling it out.*) C-A-P-P-U-C-C-I-N-O. All right. (*To Saffron.*) Oh, go on, darling, make the most of Mummy while you're still at home, before you run away to be a student.

Saffron goes to coffee machine.

Mother (*To Saffron.*) Oh, you told her, dear. Well done.

Edina Oh, God! Although why anybody wants to be a student nowadays is a mystery to me. No fun, darling, no demos, no experimental drug-taking. You're just industry fodder, darling. At least in my day, darling, people used to go to university just to close them down. What will your protest be, darling, a pair of stripey tights and some liquorice allsort earrings? Oh, wow! Call out the National Guard.

Mother (*To Saffron.*) Just jealous, dear.

Edina (*Reacting.*) I could have been a student.

Mother Oh-ho-ho. Thick as two short planks, her reports said.

Saffron goes to the fridge.

Edina It did not say that, *it did not say that.* Ask Patsy, darling. She wrote most of them.

Saffron There's no milk.

Edina Oh, no milk. Haven't Harrods been here yet, darling. They're normally here by now, aren't they?

Saffron I'll pop out and get some.

Edina Oh, no, that would be a complete waste of money.

Saffron And how would you know? When was the last time you bought a carton of milk?

Edina A carton? Now stop it. Stop getting all hung-up about money, darling. It's all pounds-shillings-and-pence to me.

Saffron It probably was the last time you had anything to do with it. The Queen carries more cash. Your whole life is on account.

Edina Oh, stop it. I'll have it black, all right.

Mother (*To Saffron.*) I'll have a black chappuccino, Saffy.

Edina (*To Mother.*) Espresso.

Mother Yes, I am in rather a hurry. As a matter of fact, I think I'd better be off. I want to catch the post.

Edina Oh, dear! What a strange archaic little world you live in, isn't it?

Saffron Bye, Gran.

Mother Bye, dear.

Edina Just leave. Oh and that reminds me, just leave and go straight out that front door. Do not go upstairs to my bedroom and steal things.

Mother (*To Saffron.*) I don't know what she's talking about. She's deranged.

Edina I passed that sad little excuse for a charity shop yesterday. I saw your little piece of handiwork in the window.

Mother looks a little guilty.

Edina Must be the only genuine Lacroix, Versace, quilty bedspread in existence.

Saffron Gran!

Mother It was in a bin-liner.

Edina (*To Saffron.*) It was my dry-cleaning, darling. (*To Mother.*) Go on, just get out.

Saffron Bye, Gran.

Mother Goodbye, dear. (*To Edina.*) Oh, by the way, if you do hit hard times and there is anything you need to sell, my friend Hermione has this little shop.

Hands Edina the card.

Edina (*Reading aloud.*) 'Bric-n-brac 'n' nic'n'nacs, things – any old junk taken'. (*To Mother.*) Why don't you trade yourself in? Get out, go on, go on.

Mother She'd give you a very good price, dear.

Edina Oh, just leave.

Mother I'm only trying to help. Arriva derky.

Saffron Bye, Gran.

Mother leaves.

Edina Gran! Gran! Mum and Gran, Mum and Gran. Mum and Gran. God, it's so depressing. It's like something out of *EastEnders*, darling, isn't it. Mum and Gran. (*The buzzer goes. She moves to press the button to open upstairs door.*) Oh, God! I'm sure you could find a more appropriate name for that thieving old person, couldn't you? Like Moomy or Nanu or old Kaka.

Patsy enters. She flies down the stairs, swearing as she goes. She is fumbling in her bag for her fags.

Patsy Light, light, light, light!

She grabs the packet and takes four or five of them and smokes them as a bunch. Edina lights one, too, blowing extra smoke in Patsy's direction.

Edina Oh dear, Pats, honestly. Not another no-smoking cab, Pats? They must see you coming these days.

Patsy Bloody bastard asthmatic cab-driver.

Edina Well, I hope you refused to pay him this time.

Saffy tuts.

Patsy It was one of your account cabs, Eds. I think you should get him fired.

BULOUS
B

Saffron Oh, so not only do you want the man to die of passive smoking, but you also want to deny him a living of any kind?

Edina (*Mockingly.*) Passive smoking? I suppose we're shortening your life, are we, darling?

Patsy If only.

Edina For your information, you have to be taking great big lung bucketfuls to make any difference.

Patsy Not little wasp breaths.

Edina No. And excuse me if I sue and I die prematurely of passive boredom, or dull-as-dishwater-daughter induced stress. All right?

Patsy Whole bloody hour it took me. I nearly didn't make it.

Edina God! Well, why didn't you use those nicotine patches I gave you for emergencies, darling?

Patsy I did. (*She opens her shirt to reveal patches stuck on every available piece of skin.*) They're all dead now. Can you get the ones off my back.

Edina (*Preparing to take one off.*) Ready?

Patsy Yeah, yeah.

Edina Go. (*Removes first patch.*)

Patsy (*Groaning.*) Uh!

Edina Ready?

Patsy Okay. Oh!

Edina Actually, most of these ones seem all right, darling. In fact, they're leeching something off your skin rather than the other way round.

Saffron She's probably recharging them.

Patsy Careful, Eddy, don't rip so hard.

Saffron Yes, careful. At her age the flesh slides off the bone like a well-cooked chicken.

ABSOLUTELY *fa*

Edina For your information, there are some people who would pay a lot of money for Patsy's body.

Saffron Morticians. How much do you think you'd get for a ready-embalmed carcass? No wonder she's always been refused a donor card.

Patsy notices Saffy's bare arm in front of her. She slaps a couple of Nicorette patches on. Edina approves.

Patsy Oh – wasp, sweetie.

There is the sound of a car horn outside.

Edina Oh, my car's here.

Patsy Oh, Eddy, I thought a little mosey down Bond Street . . . a little sniff around Gucci, sidle up to Ralph Lauren, pass through Browns and then on to Quags for a light lunch.

Edina Oooh, yum, yum, yum, yum, yum.

Saffron Tell her.

Edina (*Evasively.*) Oh, I've just got to pop in for a bit of a . . . a . . .

Saffron Mum!

Edina (*Defeated.*) I've got to meet my accountant this morning, but it won't take long, will it, sweetie?

Patsy Why?

Edina Well, because her bastard father and Marshall are trying to cut off my alimony payments, that's why.

Saffron She's been bleeding them dry for years.

Edina Whose side are you on? Do you want us to be poor?

Patsy (*Horrified.*) You'll be poor!

Saffron (*To Patsy.*) That's got you worried.

Patsy Eddy, we simply cannot allow them to cut us off like this, sweetie. Now listen, Eddy, it's not alimony, it is compensation.

Edina Yes, yes!

Saffron For what?

Patsy (*Staring at Saffron.*) Errrr . . .

Edina Yes, darling, it's damages, sweetie. For those long crippling hours of painful labour I went through on your behalf.

Saffron You had a Caesarean.

Edina Yes, I know I had a Caesarean, darling. But how do you think it feels for Mummy to wake up every morning and look down and see her stomach smiling back up at her, um? You can't put a price on that.

Saffron (*To Edina, as she makes to leave.*) Come on, let's go.

Edina Yes, let's go, darling. (*To Patsy.*) Little meeting, big lunch. Do you think Quags or Daphne's?

Patsy Oh, er, er, er, er . . . (*Juggling.*)

Edina I don't know. Either way, either way.

They exit.

scene three Interior Edina's office. Day one. Later.

Normal amount of activity in the background. Bubble is lying on the sofa with her legs flopped over the back. She is asleep. Saffron, Edina and Patsy enter through the outer office.

Edina Right, I'm here, don't panic – everything's under control.

Saffron Mum, relax. We're on time. In fact, we're a bit early.

Edina has nothing worked out for this circumstance. Patsy pours a glass of wine and sits on the sofa.

Patsy Look, Eddy, he's not here. Let's make a quick getaway before the bastard arrives.

Edina No, we can't, darling. We can't. Where's Bubble? Where's Bubble?

Patsy (*Noticing her.*) Oh, is this it? (*Indicates Bubble.*)

Edina Oh, God! Bubble, wake up Bubble. (*Shakes her.*) Come on wake up, darling. Oh – look it's like tea-break on the *Thunderbirds* set. (*Looks up.*) Somebody operate her, please!

Bubble (*Stirring.*) Oh – jeepers-creepers. Blimey – yer 'ere!

Edina Yes.

Bubble Was I asleep?

Saffron Hard to tell.

Bubble I've been here for hours. Oooh, I'll be really annoyed if I've missed lunch.

Saffron It's eleven o'clock.

Bubble (*Inevitably confused.*) It's just I'm really, really tired.

Patsy Oh, do we have to listen to all this?

Edina We've still got time on our hands now, thanks to Saff.

Bubble I turned on the, um – what'd'yer'me-call'it this morning . . .

Saffron Radio?

Bubble I want to say telephone . . . (*Mimicking picking up a telephone.*) . . . No, that's not right, that's not right. You look at it . . .

Edina . . . television.

Bubble That's it! 'Good Morning Television'. Hallo! Which I don't normally do because I find myself falling back to sleep like that . . . (*Snaps fingers.*)

Patsy Good morning television, my God. If they could market that in pill form Switzerland would be plunged into a recession.

Bubble And, anyway, they said 'Leave home now. There's a strike on the buses'. It were really urgent. So I did and I got here hours ago.

Saffron On the tube?

Bubble No, I only live down the road. I walk here. So they must be bonkers! I wonder what they're telling everyone else?

Edina Huh! Have you seen my accountant?

Saffron (*To Bubble.*) She's talking to you!

Bubble Oh! Ooh, what's he look like?

Edina Well, he looks like an accountant, sweetie, doesn't he!

Patsy (*Venomously.*) A bitter paper-pusher always dealing with salaries larger than his own and resenting every second.

Edina Um.

Bubble gets up from the sofa supporting herself on Patsy's head – squashing Patsy's hairstyle.

scene four **Interior Edina's office. Day one. Twenty minutes later.**

Malcolm, Edina's accountant, is seated at her desk. He is in his mid-thirties, grey-suited, enthusiastic. Saffron is beside him. Patsy is on the sofa. Edina enters.

Saffron Mum, come on. Let's get going. How many times can you go to the toilet?

Edina All right, all right, all right. I just had to get rid of Bubble, that's all, darling. I don't want her knowing my business.

Saffron Chance would be a fine thing. Right, sorry, Malcolm.

Edina settles at desk.

Edina Look, all I want to know is how much money I've got of my own, then make it look like less so my husbands can't cut me off. All right?

Malcolm Right! Well, first of all I think we should look at the fiscal . . .

Edina (*Flops on to the desk.*) Oh, God, I'M BORED!

Patsy Don't be intimidated, Eddy. I mean, look at him. There's nothing macho about having an 'O' Level in maths, a floppy disc and a personality by-pass. Come on, let's go to lunch.

Edina Let's go to lunch, yeah.

Saffron Mum, this meeting is for you. Malcolm has come here to talk to you, to help you. Now sit down and shut up. I'm sorry, Malcolm.

Edina (*Sits.*) Oh, oh. All right, go on.

Malcolm Well, first of all, let me say that the question of alimony is now settled.

Edina Oh, well, there we are! Come on, Pats.

Malcolm You are no longer receiving payments.

Edina What?

Patsy You bastard.

Edina They can't do that.

Saffron They have.

There is silence.

Edina Oh! (*Suspiciously.*) You knew about this, didn't you, sweetie. (*Slowly.*) Malcolm – am I *poor*?

Patsy Just yes or no.

Malcolm Let me explain . . .

Edina Oh, no.

Patsy Oh, don't explain. (*Exits.*)

Edina sits down contritely.

scene five Interior Edina's office. Day one. Ten minutes later.

Edina, Saffy and Malcolm are sitting round desk. Malcolm is speaking. Edina is very bored.

Malcolm . . . if you expend the thirty-eight per cent, then all liabilities with the necessary adjustments can be done in respect of your company, which I find rather exciting, uh, . . .

Patsy enters sniffing, crosses to the sofa and starts drinking.

Malcolm . . . however, with the accumulation of overpayments on outstanding tax liabilities, a lesser amount will be due. So . . . er . . . let's move on to the depreciation . . .

Edina Look, I just want to know how much money I've got. Why will you never tell me? Eh? I mean, I've got two businesses, haven't I?

Malcolm Oh, yes, your er 'businesses'.

Indicates quotation marks.

Edina What's that? (*Imitates his quotation marks.*) What did you do, then? What's that? This is a top PR company. There must be money in it, isn't there?

Malcolm Well, there will always be talented creative people in need of publicity . . .

Edina Oh, God – if they were talented and creative they wouldn't need me.

Patsy We're talking Planet Hollywood.

Edina Exactly.

Malcolm Unfortunately, there is not much profit showing at the moment.

ABSOLUTELY fa

Edina Oh, God! Well, what about my shop?

Malcolm Uh, uh ... We were wondering about that in the office. Ummm, yes, well, stock seems to come in, and then go out, but is never paid for.

Saffron Most of it is in our sitting-room.

Edina Oh, darling, you didn't have to tell him that. I like to think of my home as a showroom, all right?

Saffron Right, tell Mum what she could do, Malcolm. Now listen, Mum.

Malcolm Well, what you could do is sell off your 'businesses' and live quite happily on the proceeds.

Edina Are you mad? Do you mean make myself unemployed? Have you any idea what the Government does to people who are unemployed, darling? They are forced to do community service, putting loft-insulation into urine-stinking old people's homes for the incontinent.

Patsy grimaces.

Edina Well, not me, darling. No, you two conspirators can think again.

Malcolm Well, there's only one thing for it. We will have to go through your monthly bills and see where a cut could be made.

Patsy looks horrified.

Edina Uhhhhh!

scene six Interior office. Day one. Ten minutes later.

There is a large pile of bills and receipts lying on the desk. Coffee has arrived. Malcolm has taken off his jacket. Everybody is looking frantic. Patsy is hovering, looking a bit worried.

Edina (*Leafing through one pile.*) Business, business, that's my flowers, that's business.

Malcolm Pedicure and nose-plucking?

Edina Stop it! Don't look at me like that . . . It is very important for business for me to look good, and looking good costs money. I'm not like Saffy. I can't walk around looking like . . .

Patsy A stale old piece of toast.

Edina Exactly! It takes more than a cold flannel and some Body Shop oatmeal scrub for me, you know. I mean, I can't meet clients smelling like an old bowl of porridge, can I, sweetie? These are valid business expenses.

Malcolm Jit Sag?

Edina That's my shiatsu.

Malcolm Geoffrey Weinbaum?

Edina Decorator.

Malcolm Oh, yes, this one comes up again and again, Don Alphonso de Colombo. (*Edina and Patsy look guilty.*)

Edina That's er . . . wicker baskets.

Saffron (*Disgusted.*) Parasite.

Edina Just look at you! Stop getting at Patsy. It's not her fault, you know. I mean, we're both here having to do all this, darling, and he is doing nothing about this huge amount of tax I'm still having to pay.

Malcolm I am doing everything I can within the law.

Edina Oh, God, and what on earth is the point of having an accountant if he's within the law? I might just as well do it myself. In fact, I think I will. Right, I'm off.

Patsy (*To Saffron.*) Zzzzzzzzz. (*She slaps another Nicorette patch on Saffy's arm.*) Wasp sweetie!

scene seven Interior Edina's kitchen. Day two.

Justin and Saffron are in the kitchen talking, finishing off a cup of coffee. Justin is looking nervous.

Saffron She's gone to choose a smaller car. I told her to get rid of that ridiculous driver and the limo.

Justin You didn't tell her I was paying for you to go to university, did you?

Saffron I had to.

Justin Oh, no! I mean, it is all right? You know, money-wise? There's no real problem?

Saffron Dad, she's not poor. She's got more money hanging around in little schemes and investments than it's safe for her to know about. Malcolm and I just frightened her into slimming everything down a bit.

Justin Oh, she's not a great slimmer, sweetie. I mean, she could eat air and put on weight.

Saffron Yes, well, I intend to keep her thinking she's poor for a while. It may cut out the worst of her excesses.

Justin Ooh, they say all daughters turn into their mothers.

Saffron Dad!

There is the sound of someone coming down the stairs.

Justin Oh, Jesus Christ! (*Standing up in complete panic.*)

Edina Saff . . . (*Entering breezily down the stairs.*)

Saffron Dad's here. Don't forget what you agreed.

Edina (*Stopping dead for a second. Speaking very calmly.*) I am civilized to my platform toes, darling. Hallo, Justin. (*She pauses.*)

Justin Edina.

Edina Can I make you a cup of coffee from our new machine, although I don't know if there's any coffee to go in it, since Harrods no longer visits me daily. (*Saffron glares.*)

Edina The only delivery we get nowadays is from the Red Cross. Ha-ha-ha! Still, I suppose I could just go through the motions, though, you'd probably like that, Justin . . . It would be a little bit . . .

Justin and Edina . . . like our marriage.

They both laugh falsely.

Edina Oh . . . (*To Saffron.*) Isn't it rather lovely for you, darling, to see Mummy and Daddy sharing a joke like that. Is it, sweetie? Um?

Justin I'm really glad you're taking this so well.

Saffron goes to the fridge and is hidden from view for two seconds. The tension mounts between Edina and Justin, and unable to contain her fury, Edina grabs hold of him.

Edina I just can't bloody believe that you are cutting me off . . . just so you can send *that* to Further Education. What kind of father are you? (*Saffron reappears and Edina sings.*) La-la-la-la-la. Hi, darling. Patsy and I are off shopping. (*Shouts.*) Pats.

Patsy enters.

Patsy Just . . .

Justin Pats.

Saffron (*To Edina.*) Did you get a smaller car?

Edina Yes, miniscule, darling.

Patsy Practically a bicycle.

Edina (*Indicating something very small.*) It's this big, it's this big.

Saffron Here's the list.

Edina (*Mockingly.*) Here's the list. Shopping-list. Shopping-list for Mum. Thank you, darling. Milk . . . Milk. Where am I supposed to go for milk?

Patsy Food Hall, on the left, past the fish.

Edina Yeah. Well, if we're going to the Food Hall, we might as well get the lot there.

Saffron You can't get the food shopping from Harrods.

Patsy Of course you can. You can't expect people who live in Knightsbridge to eat out all the time.

Saffron Go to the supermarket.

Edina The what, darling?

scene eight Exterior Edina's house. Day two.

At the door we see Patsy, Edina and Saffron. Edina is carrying a pathetically small shopping basket. She says goodbye to Saffron.

Edina (*Reading list.*) Supermarket shopping for Mum. Eggs, cod steaks, apples for Saffy. Eggs, cod steaks, apples for Saffy ... right ... er ...

Saffron (*Appalled.*) That's not the car?

Edina and Patsy are getting into a spanking new Alfa Romeo Spider.

Edina Smallest one I could find, darling. It's tiny, look. There's barely room for the basket in here, darling. No room for you, I'm afraid. I told you so, unless Patsy wants you on her knees. (*To Patsy.*) Do you, darling? No? (*To Saffron.*) She doesn't want you, darling. Safety first. Bye, sweetie.

They drive off erratically.

scene nine Day two. Driving sequence.

The car swerves at speed. Patsy and Edina are singing inside.

Edina/Patsy 'Welcome to the Hotel California ... It's such a lovely place, such a lovely place ...'

scene ten Driving sequence. Day two. Two minutes later.

They are driving at speed.

Edina Come on, darling, let's have the roof off.

Patsy Oh, yeah – it's too bloody hot in here.

Edina unclips the roof and starts to lift it back, but Patsy's hair is caught in it.

Patsy (*Shrieking in pain.*) Ow! Ow! Pull over, Ed – pull over, Ed, pull over, pull over, my hair, my hair. Ow! That's better.

scene eleven Driving sequence. Day two. Moments later.

The car goes through a red traffic light.

Patsy Go for it, Eddy!

Edina accelerates.

scene twelve Driving sequence. Day two.

They have stopped at a pedestrian crossing, tooting at people to get out of the way.

Edina (*To shocked pedestrians.*) What? Come on! It's a road – it's a road!

scene thirteen Driving sequence. Day two.

Edina is trying to turn round, blocking traffic, oblivious to the problem she is creating. A woman in a car behind shakes her head in a very patronizing way.

Edina There's a supermarket down here. There used to be a supermarket here . . .

Woman in the car behind sounds her horn.

Edina (*To woman.*) What? What? Come on!

Edina and Patsy get out and tackle her, hitting her car.

Edina Don't you shake your head at me!

Patsy (*To woman.*) Errr? Watch your language! Watch your foul language. You cow! Come on Eddy, let's just go.

The woman writes down their number.

scene fourteen Interior supermarket. Day two.

Patsy and Edina walking around in shock. They have never been in a supermarket before. Edina is looking at her list.

Edina (*Seeking help.*) Hallo? (*Nobody responds.*) Take a trolley, Pats. Bring a trolley.

Both push around a huge trolley.

Edina Oh, God!

Edina goes to the margarine section and is overwhelmed. She piles far too much into the trolley. As they proceed they fill up third trolley.

Patsy (*Arriving at drinks section.*) Here we are, Ed.

Edina Darling, I just can't push any more.

Patsy But sweetie . . .

Edina I haven't got the strength, darling – come on. God damn it.

Patsy cannot restrain herself at the drinks section and secretly takes a swig of vodka from one of the bottles on the shelf.

scene fifteen Interior supermarket. Day two: at the check-out.

Standing at the check-out, Edina has no idea what to do.

Edina (*Indicating trolleys to the check-out woman.*) It's all three – all three here, all right?

Patsy arrives clutching a crate of champagne.

Patsy (*Pleading.*) Eddy – Eddy – please, please, please, please, please, please.

Edina I can't afford champagne. (*She indicates that Patsy should put it* on the rack under the trolley, so it can't be seen.) Put it underneath. (*To the check-out woman.*) Just the weekly shop for me this ... A working mum!

scene sixteen Driving around Harvey Nichols. Day two.

They are driving round and round looking for somewhere to park.

Edina Oh – nowhere to park.

Patsy Eddy, we've been round four times.

Edina I'm just going to put it in here. (*Drives up on to pavement outside main entrance.*) Just going to put it in.

Patsy It'll just go here.

Edina That's okay.

Patsy I mean, we won't be here all day. All right.

Edina They know me here.

Patsy There's a bar on the fifth floor.

Edina Yes, we might start there. Hang on, darling. Let me put my shoes on.

scene seventeen Exterior Harvey Nichols. Day two: later.

As Patsy and Edina leave Harvey Nichols, they do not notice immediately that the car has been clamped.

Edina Darling – you have to slow down while I'm walking in these shoes.

Patsy (*Noticing wheel clamp.*) Eddy – what's this? What's this? What is this?

Edina (*Puzzled.*) Darling – has that been there all the time? Who put this thing on?

Patsy What is it?

scene eighteen Interior underground car pound. Day two.

Edina and Patsy stagger in.

Edina God, why does it have to be in some underground shame-hole, like this? Is this the car-clamp club?

They go to a payment booth and Edina immediately starts to complain.

Edina You put this on my car. It's a clamp, all right? I mean, I left it there for ten minutes. Do you understand, ten minutes. Until I get that car insured – it's a very expensive car – I have to park it where I can see it. Do you understand me?

A whole row of very expensively dressed men and women are all doing exactly the same.

Edina What do you mean I have to wait for my car for two or three hours. What am I going to do in two bloody hours, um? Um?

The people in the booths are unmoved. They've heard it all before. There is the relentless sound of cash-tills ringing.

scene nineteen Driving sequence. Day two.

They are speeding again, and are being followed by the police.

Edina (*Trying to wave them by.*) Come by – come by. What? What? What? What? What?

Policeman Could you step out of the car, please, madam.

Edina gets out, incensed.

Edina I mean, what the hell...

They are both obviously drunk. Patsy tries to get out clutching a bottle of champagne. Edina falls at the policeman's feet in a drunken stupor.

Patsy You pig! What do you want? What are you doing to her?

Edina I'm just taking my friend to hospital. She's sick.

Patsy Eddy I'll ... help. Hang on.

The scene fades.

scene twenty Interior small courtroom. Day three.

Edina is sitting next to lawyer, with Patsy and Saffron behind. They are looking up to the judge and the magistrate who is reading out the list of charges.

Judge Driving without a licence, driving without insurance, not wearing a seatbelt, having no tax disc displayed, driving over the legal speed limit, driving under the influence of alcohol, allowing another person to drive your vehicle under the influence of alcohol. In the region of £5,000 of parking fees owing, £6,000 of damage to property. Charges of assault, and abuse. The charges of attempted murder and robbery have been dropped. Shoplifting...

Patsy (*To judge.*) My name is Patsy Stone. I'm an alcoholic, and what she did was an act of humanitarian mercy.

Judge That is hardly a reason to steal a crate of champagne.

Edina Have you any idea how much champagne costs these days? I was forced to steal it. My daughter wouldn't have allowed me to buy it.

Judge I must ask you to sit down and stop wasting the court's time ... The sum of £50,000 is to be paid by you in damages, and a further fine of £2,000. You will also be liable for all costs incurred.

Edina (*To Saffron.*) Well, getting rid of my driver was a little bit of a false economy, wasn't it, sweetie?

Judge ... and a lifetime ban on driving. And finally Mrs Monsoon...

Edina Can I just say one word in my defence ... Um?...

Saffron I don't think that's a good idea, Mum. Your mouth is working for the prosecution.

Edina Oh, darling, this is what I do well, sweetie. You might pick up a few tips for the Debating Society, darling, you never know. Without notes, Saff (*Mother claps.*) Thank you, thank you. (*To judge.*) Right – I the proposed accused think that, well I mean, you know, well the day in question was not a good day for me, all right? But I put it to you that I don't see how any day could have been good the way this bloody country's run. Well, you know, I was just trying to do my best, trying to get from A to B, do a little shopping. I was trying to take control of my life, you know, only to find that actually it's controlled for me by petty bureaucracy and bits of bloody paper, ignorant bloody petty rules and laws that just obstruct every tiny little action until you find you've committed a crime without even knowing it. I mean, you know, why can't life just be made a little easier for everybody, eh? Why can't it be more like the Continent, um? You know, where a man can just park his car on the pavement and then run down the street in front of charging bulls while letting fireworks off out of his bloody nostrils without anyone blinking an eye? Uh? Because it's probably a local holiday and nobody's at work because they all want to have just a little bit of fun and they're not intimidated by some outdated work ethic. I mean, there has to be more to life than just being safe . . .

Judge Is there a point to all this?

Edina Yes. Yes! Why, oh why, do we pay taxes, um? I mean, just to have bloody parking restrictions and buggery-ugly traffic wardens, and bollocky-pedestrian-bloody-crossings, and those bastard railings outside shops, so you can't even get in them? I mean, I know they are there to stop stupid people running into the street and killing themselves, but we're not all stupid, we don't all need nursemaiding. I mean, why not just have a 'Stupidity Tax', just tax the stupid people.

Patsy (*Stands up.*) Let them die!

Edina Yes!

Judge Any more of this ridiculous rant and I'll put you both away . . .

Mother Hear, hear.

Judge Edina Margaret Rose Monsoon, I hereby sentence you to . . .

Credits.

scene twenty-one Exterior old-people's home. Day four.

Patsy and Eddy are standing clutching a huge roll of loft-insulation. They knock at the door, and an old woman opens it.

Edina Community service.

Old Lady Oh! Oh, you've come to do the loft. Come in.

Edina (*To old woman.*) It's all your bloody fault, you know, this.

Freeze frame as Patsy and Edina move inside and get their first whiff.

Cast List

Edina · JENNIFER SAUNDERS
Patsy · JOANNA LUMLEY
Saffron · JULIA SAWALHA
Mother · JUNE WHITFIELD
Patsy's Mother · ELEANOR BRON
Justin · CHRISTOPHER MALCOLM
Fireman · WOLF CHRISTIAN
Nurse (Edina's birth) · JANE GALLOWAY
Nurse (Saffy's birth) · SUZY AITCHISON
Writer · PHILIP FRANKS
Dancer · MARY MACKENZIE
Guitar Player · MIA SOTERIOU

scene one Interior Edina's hallway. Day one.

It is early morning. Suddenly the fire alarm goes off. Saffy appears at the top of stairs. Smoke starts to drift up from the kitchen.

Saffron (*Runs downstairs and picks up portable phone on the table, dialling 999.*) Fire! Mum, wake up, fire! (*On telephone.*) Yes, hallo, fire service, please. It's 34 Claremont Avenue, London, W11 4BX. Thank you. (*Edina enters.*) Come on, Mum. Let's wait outside.

Edina Oh, oh, oh, oh. (*Runs upstairs to bedroom followed by Saffy.*)

scene two Interior Edina's bedroom.

Edina is frantically sorting clothes out at her wardrobe. Saffy enters.

Saffron Mum, come on, please. There's a fire in the kitchen.

Edina I'm trying to put something on, sweetie.

Saffron We're going to die if we don't get out now. It doesn't matter what you wear. Come on.

Edina Oh, God, I just hate all my clothes. Why have I never got anything to wear. What shall I put on? What, what, what shall I put on? I'm just fat, fat, fat. Why won't my cells stop dividing and multiplying?

Saffron Mum, there is a fire downstairs . . .

A fireman enters the room.

Fireman Come on, ladies. We have to evacuate the building. You must leave now.

Edina That's easy for you to say. You've got a uniform. You know what you're going to wear each day. It's harder for me.

scene three Interior Edina's hallway.

Edina and Saffron watch glumly as the firemen roll up their hoses, pack up and leave. The firemen coming up from the kitchen are wearing breathing apparatus. The fire obviously started there.

ABSOLUTELY fa

Edina (*To nearest fireman.*) It's nice that uniform ... Where do you get those uniforms?

Fireman (*Not hearing.*) Well, I reckon that's about it, then.

Saffron What do you think could have caused it?

Fireman Could have been a cigarette.

Edina Patsy!

Saffron Where was she?

Edina looks ominously towards the stairs.

Edina Down there! (*Indicating the kitchen.*) Where's she gone, darling? She can't be down there. She could never let six grown men out alive. She can't be here ...

scene four Interior Edina's blackened burnt-out kitchen.

Edina and Saffron make their way down the charred staircase. The kitchen is a write-off. The only recognizable feature is the table, which is blackened and still slightly smoking.

Saffron (*Aghast.*) Oh!

Edina Oh! Oh, God ... Patsy?

As Edina cries out, a charred lump that is Patsy rises up from her normal place at the table. She is all black, but for a small patch of face she has been lying on. A fag is still smouldering in her mouth.

Saffron She's inhaled our kitchen.

Patsy I just ... um ... I just nodded off ... um ...

scene five Interior Edina's bedroom. Day two.

It is Japanese-style. Edina is clearing out her wardrobe, putting clothes in piles. Saffron enters.

Saffron Hallo.

Edina Shoes off, sweetie. Sit–sit–sit. Hallo, darling.

Saffron You should do something about Patsy.

Edina What do you mean, darling?

Saffron Send her to a clinic or something before she kills us all.

Edina Sweetie, she's been to a clinic, and dried out. They didn't have enough room for all the toxic waste they pumped out of her. Even Japan refused to take it. She's been dried out, darling, and it made absolutely no difference.

scene six Interior Edina's hallway. Flashback early 1980s.

Edina opens the front door, and Patsy jogs in, looking quite unlike her normal self – healthy, clear-headed, smiling, cheerful. She is just out of the detox clinic.

Edina Pats.

Patsy (*Springing in, full of life.*) Oh, hallo, Eddy. It's such a *beautiful* day out there. You know, the sun's so bright it's almost blinding, like shards of glass just piercing the clouds. Oh, every second of my journey here is emblazoned on my memory. I feel fantastic.

Edina Champagne!

Patsy (*Immediately relapsing.*) Oh, yeah. I think so. Oh, Eddy.

Edina has a bottle ready opened. Patsy drinks like there is no tomorrow.

scene seven Interior Edina's bedroom. Day two.

Saffron and Edina are sorting through clothes.

Edina If Pats wanted to do something about it, darling, she would. Now give me a little hand here, would you.

Saffron What are you doing?

Edina Well, I'm throwing out all my clothes, of course.

Saffron Why?

Edina For insurance ... um, it's fire damage all this, sweetie. Fire damage, darling.

Saffron Well, I could take these down to the charity shop.

Edina Huh! You cannot give these sort of clothes to the poor! Well, I'm sure they've got enough to contend with, without the added humiliation of wearing last-season, sweetie.

Saffron You haven't worn a lot of these. Why would you buy something and then not wear it?

Edina I don't know, darling. What is this the Krypton factor? Shall I do the obstacle course now?

Saffron Have you made a decision about the kitchen yet?

Edina No, but I want to change it – don't you? I was bored with the old ... ow! (*Trips up.*) They can bloody do this room when they're at it. I hate Japanese now.

Saffron But this was your dream! I wondered how long it would last.

Edina I'm just fed up with stubbing my toe on everything, sweetie, and going down on a futon is one thing, but getting up is quite another, darling. It's just lucky everything's at ground level, so, look, I can get to it by just rolling, sweetie. Look! (*She rolls across the room.*) Oh! oh! Help your mum up ... Help Mum up.

Saffron Um! You're going out tonight, aren't you?

Edina Yes.

Saffron Good, because I've got friends coming round.

Edina Oh, then definitely, sweetie.

Saffron We've got to watch a documentary on TV.

Edina Oh, all right. (*Notices something about Saffy.*) What is it that's different about you today? Hum? What is it? There's a top button left open on your – what are we calling this – blouse ... is it, sweetie, blouse? (*Looks at Saffy's breasts.*) Have your shoulder pads slipped?

Saffron Oh, stop it.

Edina There's nothing to be ashamed of. You're getting a bit of a big girl, aren't you, darling? (*Buzzer goes downstairs.*) Oh, that'll be the bike with the swatches. I'd better go down . . . the front door's buggered. And don't you take any of those clothes off to the homeless while I'm downstairs. I haven't forgotten, darling, that time I was accosted by that mentally deranged down-and-out who leapt out of a cardboard box wearing a Vivienne Westwood catsuit and Chanel suede mules. I still haven't recovered from that, sweetie.

Saffron Only because *he* looked better in them.

Edina Oh! (*Makes a raspberry noise.*)

scene eight Interior sitting-room. Day two. Ten minutes later.

The room is a little more crammed than usual. Some of the items rescued from the kitchen are there, glasses, crockery, etc., and some charred bits and pieces. Mother is there wiping soot off some plates. Edina is flicking through magazines and decoration books. Saffron is there, too, sorting out some lecture notes.

Edina I just like them all, sweetheart. Every picture in here I like . . . I want, I want. Every picture in here, sweetie. I mean, I want people to think I'm *all* these types of things. You know, sweetie. I mean I know it should reflect my personality but . . .

Saffron God forbid.

Edina Sweetie, this is it style-wise. Look at this, sweetie, Irish crofters' cottage. Umm . . . umm . . . umm . . . umm . . . um?

Saffron Mum, it's a kitchen . . . It needs a cooker, not peat-fired oven.

Edina (*Turns TV on.*) Oh, I can't be bothered to think about it now anyway.

Saffron Well, when? (*Turns TV off.*) We can't go on living in this room like this.

ABSOLUTELY fa

Edina Not big enough for you, sweetie. Let me see what I can do. (*Gets up and tries pushing the walls to make the house bigger.*) Oh hang on – oh! oh, this is as big as it gets I'm afraid, darling. What do you mean it's just not big enough when you want to hog the whole room with your lichen friends and watch some dull nil-rated narrated doco.

Saffron Oh, stop it.

Mother I rather like living like this. It's a bit like the war, dear.

Edina What do you mean, it's a bit like the war?

Saffron Leave it, Mum.

Edina Well, what does she mean? 'It's a bit like the war.' It's a bit like the war, but without the drab fashion, the powdered eggs, the rationing, the bombing, in fact without the war. Yeah, a bit like the war but, *without the war.*

Saffron You always have to say something. Why can't you let anything just go by?

Edina I can. (*Turns on TV again.*)

Saffron Mum, I want Channel Four. You are going out, aren't you? (*No response.*) Mum!

Edina Am I allowed to open my mouth? (*Mouths.*) Am I allowed to open my mouth? 'Cos if I am, then yes. I'm going out when Patsy gets here. All right? Oh, it's just the news on this one, sweetie. Can't we have MTV?

Saffron No, I don't want to miss it.

Mother What's it about, dear?

Saffron Well, in layman's terms, Gran . . .

Edina Sex, is it?

Saffron The beginnings of life – conception to birth.

Mother Oh, birth. That's changed so much since my day.

Edina What do you mean it's changed?

Saffron Mum!

Mother Oh, yes, they'd whip you into hospital, no questions asked, and take your tonsils out as a precaution.

Saffron We're much more relaxed these days.

Edina We are? Are we? Are we?

Mother In my day, they could incarcerate you in a high-security asylum just for not having a whiter-than-white wash.

Saffron (*Thinks she's joking.*) Gran!

Mother Yes, dear, and in those days it was the bromide sedatives or ECT.

Saffron What's ECT?

Mother Electric shock treatment. It's all highly addictive. I still can't pass a plug socket without getting the urge to put my finger in.

Edina Well, I wish you would. (*To Saffron.*) Don't be so impressed with her anyway, sweetie, darling. Don't be so impressed, sweetie, darling, sweetie, darling, sweetie, darling, sweetie, darling, sweetie, darling, sweetie, darling. You don't mind me calling you that, do you? Sweetie, eh, darling? I don't know how it started, but it's hard to break a habit like that after so many years.

Saffron It started because you couldn't remember my name for the first three years.

Edina Don't be ridiculous, darling! You didn't have a name for the first four, did she? 'Thing', 'thing', 'it'. (*Notices Saffy laying out nibbles.*) Kettle crisps? Kettle crisps? You don't normally have kettle crisps for your friends, do you? It's normally some dried old pumpkin seeds and a small pack of Golden Wonder, isn't it?

Mother I think I can feel one of my heads coming on, dear. Have you any aspirin? Or that homophobic remedy you gave me last time was good.

Saffron Homoeopathic. I'll get them. (*Exits.*)

ABSOLUTELY fab

Edina (*To Mother.*) You knew that. We're not amused. Anyway, what are you doing? What are you still doing here?

Mother Well, I'm just keeping Saffy company, dear.

Edina Well, she doesn't need your sort of 'old woman' company. You're a burden to her, you know. You should get out and hang out with some people of your own age for once. And hopefully she'll get horribly lonely and find a life. All right?

Saffron returns with a box of homoeopathic remedies in bottles. She opens one, then another, then another. They are all empty.

Saffron Why are these all empty? They were in your room. (*Looks to Edina.*)

Edina I was very sick last night, darling.

Saffron All of them! (*Goes on staring at Edina.*)

Edina Well, I was hungry. I mean, I ... It's the only thing I could find that didn't have calories in it. I mean, what's the problem?

Patsy (*Entering.*) Eddy?

Edina Ah, here she is.

Saffron Ah, here she is. The human barbecue.

Patsy Are we going out, Eddy?

Edina Yeah, do you want a little drink or something though first, Pats?

Saffron sighs.

Patsy Oh, yeah.

Patsy and Edina sit, pour themselves a drink and crack open a pack of crisps, much to Saffy's annoyance.

Mother I think I'll pop off, dear. I'll just nip off home and get an aspirin.

Saffron Okay, Gran.

Edina Good.

Saffron (*To Mother.*) Um . . . you have to actually pull the door hard and lock it with the key until we get it replaced.

Mother I think I can manage that. (*She exits.*)

She exits, closing the door behind her. At that moment Saffy notices that Patsy has changed TV channels and a tussle begins for the remote control.

Patsy Ahh–Ahh!

Edina (*To Saffy.*) Give it to her. (*Patsy wins back the control and she and Eddy sit back to watch TV.*)

Edina (*To Patsy.*) Oh it's *Top of the Pops*, darling. Have we got time to watch the Pops, sweetie?

Patsy Yeah, there's no rush.

Saffron Mum, you can't stay. You promised.

Edina Oh, we'll be going in a minute, sweetie. (*Continues to watch TV with Patsy.*) Oh, what's happened to this programme anyway? Can't they find anyone to present it who doesn't look like a mannequin from Next children's department? Simon Mayo!

Patsy The bands are just second-rate crap bands that I didn't like the first time around.

Edina I know! I wish someone would shoot Genesis! Look at them.

Patsy I know, evil-looking creeps just playing dull soulless dance music . . . bip-bip-bip-bip-bip-bip-bip-bip-bip-bip-bop.

Saffron You're showing your age.

Edina God, well I hate all this 70s' revival crap as well.

Patsy Yeah, it's just watered-down crap.

Edina Well, look at Lenny Kravitz there at number thirty. Thinks he's Jimmy-bloody-Hendrix.

Patsy The genius of Jimmy Hendrix was that he could stand up at all . . . He was so pumped full of so many drugs.

Edina Exactly, exactly. He might have choked and died at any second. That was the thrill.

Patsy Who dies in their own vomit these days?

Edina No one.

Patsy No one.

Edina Mind you, I wish some of them would, though. You know, I don't think that 'Kylie Minogue chokes on vegetarian sausage after all-night-not-drinking binge in safe celebrity night spot' has quite the same ring about it somehow. (*To Saffron.*) Sorry, I know you like her. I know you like her; I'm sorry about that, darling, but you can't play rock-and-roll on a diet of Quorn, Vegejuice and Linda-bloody-McCartney's Tofu Treats. I've seen the ones you've got in the fridge anyway, darling. (*To Patsy.*) It's all getting out of control all these revivals. Isn't it, revivals? They're not revivals. I mean, soon we'll be reviving what we had on last week!

Saffron looks anxiously at her watch.

Patsy Get your clothes back from the dry-cleaners and it's revival!

Edina I know. It's ridiculous! Just this endless stream of music, music, old music, new music, old music, new music, fashion, fashion, music, music, music, music, ... God, it's like a mirrorball spinning around in my head. Why won't it just stop?

Saffron For most people at your age it does.

Edina Switch it off, sweetie.

Patsy Yeah, give me the Stones any day, Eddy.

Edina Yes, the Stones. Yeah, yeah.

Patsy Hey, Eddy, Eddy, Eddy. You remember that weekend, with Mick and the boys? Woah-ho!

Edina Yes, fabulous days. (*To Saffron.*) Pats used to go out with Keith Moon, sweetie.

Patsy Yes, well sort of. You know, I woke up underneath him in a hotel bedroom once.

Edina That was going steady for the 60s, believe me.

Saffron Look, Mum, if you're not watching TV, can you just go?

Edina What is your problem? Uh? What is your problem? It's not as if you've gotta get rid of mother so you can have your boyfriend round, is it? I mean, we'd be out of here like a shot if there was a chance of you having a heavy snogging session on the sofa ... (*She suddenly realizes what is going on.*) Kettle crisps! Top button!

Saffron blushes. Edina is shocked.

Edina You have, haven't you, sweetie – haven't you?

Saffron (*Embarrassed.*) Mum, don't! I've got to make a phone call.

Edina No-no-no-no-no! Oh, my God, I think I'm having a palpitation. (*To Patsy.*) She's scored, she's scored. (*To Saffron.*) Patsy and I will go as soon as he gets here, sweetie.

Saffron (*Panicking.*) No, I don't want you to meet him.

Edina All right, all right, we'll go now. We're going now. C'mon get out, Pats. Move out the room, Pats. Move, sweetie, move out the room slowly, slowly. Don't frighten Saffy. Don't frighten Saffy. Just go to the door, go to the door. (*To Saffron.*) Sofa? Some crisps? Undo – undo your buttons. (*To Patsy.*) Just open the door, open the door, Pats.

Patsy gets to the door, tries to open it, but can't. It is locked.

Patsy It's stuck. It's stuck.

Saffron It's locked.

Edina That stupid bloody woman!

Saffron It's not her fault.

Edina Well, the door didn't lock itself, did it?

Saffron She just misunderstood which door I meant.

Patsy What's happened?

Edina We're locked in, Patsy.

Patsy No, no, no, no!

Edina Mind out the way. I'll do it. Mind out the way . . . Here we go.

Edina starts trying the door maniacally. She and Patsy then try to shoulder the door.

Saffron It opens inwards!

Edina Leave it, Pats. Leave it, leave it.

Patsy But how long is she going to be? She might not come back at all . . . or what if there's a fire?

Saffron She just went to get an aspirin.

Edina (*Picking up phone.*) The phone's dead, darling . . . The phone's dead . . .

Saffron (*Glaring at Patsy.*) Yes, well, the fire knocked that out.

Edina Don't look at Patsy like that. Jesus Christ, the amount you forgive that old woman. She's the one that locked us in here, sweetie.

Patsy We wouldn't even be here if you hadn't been planning your disgusting bloody snogging session on the sofa with your lover boy.

Saffron Shut up.

Edina Don't tell her to shut up. She's just trying to be nice! Come on, sweetie . . . It's all right. Come on, sweetie, you know . . . Don't get so uptight, you know. We can talk about it. Don't be so embarrassed.

Saffron Oh, stop it.

Edina Oh God!

Patsy How long is it going to take that old woman to score a tab of aspirin?

Edina I could score acid quicker.

scene nine Interior Edina's sitting-room. Day two. Half an hour later.

They are still trapped in the room. Saffron is sitting, looking upset and rejected.

Edina (*To Saffron.*) If there's anything you want, darling . . . you know, if you want to use my bedroom, feel free, sweetie, I don't mind. You know if he wants a . . . (*Blows two raspberries.*) condom, or anything, or . . .

Patsy . . . a blindfold.

Edina (*To Patsy.*) How come she gets a date, anyway? I don't get dates any more. You get dates, don't you, Pats?

Patsy Oh, I get dates, yeah.

Saffron Only if she pays the right price.

Edina (*Sidling up to Saffron.*) Do you want a little nibble, sweetie? Bombay Mix? Listen to Mummy's funny voice doing that one again. Huh? Bombay Mix, sweetie? Why didn't you tell me about him, sweetie?

Saffron Because I didn't want you to know about it, all right.

Edina I'm your friend . . .

Saffron No!

Patsy I'm your friend, Eddy. You don't need her.

Edina (*To Saffron.*) It's just that — have you any idea how exciting this is for me, darling?

Saffron (*Wearily.*) Yes.

Edina Well, I just think that it's my duty to guide you through your first sexual experience, darling. I mean, you know the facts of life, don't you — I did, I did tell you the facts of life, didn't I, sweetie?

Saffron If you mean that time that you sat on my bed and shook me awake at two o'clock in the morning, stoned out of your brain, and

then slurred into my ear 'By the way, sweetie, people have it off', then, yes, you told me the facts of life.

Edina (*Relieved.*) Well, if there are any gaps you want me to fill in, just say, sweetie. Oh, God!

Saffron (*Realizing her programme is on.*) Oh, Mum! I need to watch that programme.

Edina Oh no, darling – it's not the documentary, is it, sweetie? We can't watch that. I mean Claire Rayner narrating the journey of the sperm.

Patsy It's like watching a cookery demonstration by Hannibal Lecter.

Edina Yeah I know. I can't watch that, darling. No way. No, darling. Darling, if you want to learn about that sort of thing, you should do it like every other normal girl.

Saffron How?

Edina *Cosmo* sex quiz, sweetie. Come on, sweetie. *Cosmo* sex quiz, sweetie.

Edina We'll, we'll do it together, darling, sweetie. We'll do it together. Come on, Mum and daughter will do it together . . . Shall we, sweetie? (*They sit down together.*) Here it is. It's multiple choice, darling, all right? A, B or C? A: Is he shaggible, B: Are you shagging or C: Have you shagged? That's a nil-rating for that one, for you, isn't it? (*To Patsy.*) What other advice can we give her, darling? Uh?

Patsy Be careful of wigs.

Edina You don't need to know that one, sweetie. You don't need to know that one. Always get their number 'cos he'll never call you back. That's a good one that. B: Snogging . . . Uh – I don't like snogging. I'm not much of an expert on snogging, darling. I had two husbands – one was too short, one was gay. But still, sweetie, if you want to know how to peck a dwarf on the cheek as he's walking out the house to a disco wearing your dress, then I'm your girl!

Saffron, beginning to cry, crosses to the window.

Patsy Ignore her, Eddy.

Edina Oh, God – she's like some emotional yo-yo. You're upset, sweetie? (*To Patsy.*) She's crying, crying. (*To Saffron.*) I'm upset too, sweetie. Mummy's upset as well. (*Silence.*) Give me a hug, darling. (*They hug each other.*) Oh, oh, squish squish, squish squish, squish squish. Oh, squish squish. (*Pretending to cry too. Saffron glares at her.*) Oh, I, I can't do that thing you do . . . I can't do that tears thing you do, darling. Squish, squish, squish, squish. Come on, don't go all silent on me, darling. Come on? Where's that horrible little budgerigar girl? God! Are you all right?

Saffron pulls herself away and walks back to chair.

Saffron I will be.

Edina Well, what can I do?

Saffron Nothing, I'm okay.

Patsy Miserable little turnip.

Edina (*To Saffron.*) It's a good sign, you know.

Saffron What?

Edina It's a good sign that you're crying, sweetie. You should get in touch with your feelings more often, you know.

Saffron I *am* in touch with them, Mum. I'm not the one who has to pay £3,000 for a weekend workshop for some cross-legged conman with a red dot on his forehead to tweeze them out for me.

Edina Conman? Sher Abu Korma, darling, is a genuine reincarnation of Abu Babu high priest to the Spiritual leader Sag Aloo. Besides, I've checked. He doesn't keep all the money for himself you know. Half of it goes to the re-birthing centre and half of it goes to pay off the debts he ran up in a previous life. All right. (*Saffron still looks doubtful.*) There's a vegetarian lunch included in that price as well, don't forget that. God, honestly! Look, look, look at what you've made me do. Look, look at this . . . (*She curls up on the sofa.*) You've made me go foetal. Look, look I've gone all foetal. Look. Err, err – Mama. I'll be re-birthing soon. Actually you should try that, darling. Re-birthing, yeah.

Patsy That she was born once is enough for me.

Edina (*Starting to pant.*) Oh, here I go, sweetie, he   I go, darling.
This is all your fault, darling. Down through all those tubes . . . hallo
organs, hallo ovaries.

scene ten Flashback 1950s cold sterile hospital room. Edina's birth.

*Mother is in a little bedjacket, reading a magazine. She looks immaculate,
with beautifully set hair. She is wearing rubber gloves. The nurse gently dabs
her brow.*

Nurse (*To Mother.*) Just one last little cough for me, mummy-to-be.

Mother (*Cough-cough.*)

*There is the sound of forceps and lots of metal objects being clanked. A baby
cries.*

Nurse There we are now, untouched by human hand.

Mother puts down her magazine and waves. The scene fades.

scene eleven Interior Edina's sitting-room. Day two. Later.

Edina is lying on sofa, finishing her re-birth.

Edina (*Struggling frantically.*) Ooh, gonna have to wake me. Ooh,
where am I? Clunk-clunk-clunk-clunk. Oh, oh, it's those lights.
Oh, yeah, . . . (*Referring to Mother.*) . . . that woman's got a lot to
answer for. She'd make Eraserhead look like Emmerdale-bloody-
Farm. She didn't take her rubber gloves off for the first twelve years.
I mean, then it was just injections, injections, chemicals, chemicals,
polio, vaccine, vaccine, vaccine, bottled chemicals, bottled chemicals.
My generation made ICI what it is today, darling. No wonder we
turned to flower-power.

Saffron Well, at least Gran loved you, Mum. I know you never
wanted me. I know I was a mistake.

Patsy Pretty accurate so far.

Edina You're not a mistake, sweetie. You're just a little miscalculation, yeah, but, I mean, it doesn't matter now, sweetie. It doesn't make any difference now, sweetie.

Saffron Mum! The difference between knowing that you're wanted and knowing that you are not is quite big, you know. It's like going to a party where you know you're not invited, no matter how polite people are.

Edina Oh – she's saying very clever things now, very clever things. I suppose you think you've gate-crashed my party, is that it, darling?

Saffron I know I did.

Patsy Oh, you little bitch-troll from hell. You mean, ungrateful little bit of dirt. You think you've had it so hard. *I* never had the things you had when I was born.

Saffron Oh, here we go.

Patsy No! I never never had friends or parties or present. You know, the first few years of my life I was just locked in a room, or just trailing along behind my mother in her sickening musk-laden wake, just hoping that one day she'd just turn round and notice me, just say something to me, touch me, or ask me something, or . . .

Edina Send you to school . . .

Patsy Yeah, anything. My mother didn't give birth – she had something removed.

scene twelve Flashback Patsy's birth.

Bohemian garret in Paris 1947. Patsy's mother is sprawled on cushions dramatically giving birth. There is a writer present narrating throughout the birth, a singer singing it, a painter painting it, and an avant-garde dancer dancing it.

Writer Nous sommes, quelques amis et moi, dans une salle enfumée. Une musique! L'ambience est celle de tout les soirs, mi-amusée, mi-sceptique. Je suis gai car je viens de parler à un camarade forte bête. Je ne suis pas ivre puisque la menace du monde extérieur est toujours présente à mon esprit au lieu de cette brusque confiance qui restaure l'alcool. Apparemment, mon voisin de droite connaît la jeune fille qui a frappé mon attention. De son côté, elle semble avoir compris qu'elle a en moi un spectateur attentif. L'amour est enfant de bohême qui n'a jamais connu de lois. Si tu ne m'aimes pas je t'aime et si je t'aime prends garde à toi.

Patsy's Mother Behold, I am that which must overcome itself again and again. (*Puffs frantically at a cigarette and swigs some brandy.*) Ow! Oh! Je suis au zenith! Come, come now. Claw your way out of my body, alien soul. Who has ears to hear, let him hear! (*Falls back against the cushions and starts to push.*) Je suis Troyen, je suis de Troie! I have ploughed ... Let the swamp-blood flow forth. Yes, come now, enter the world. You tiny mediocrity, petite void, pallid horror. (*She is pushing hard, and the dancer is with her.*) Ha-oh-ow-oh-ow! Come. Come. Rip it from me. Let me be free! Cut the cord, cut the cord, cut the cord. It's draining my energy. Let it trail no longer my ball and chain. Ah! (*Patsy is born.*) What kind is it, huh?

The dancer takes the baby and dances with it.

Writer C'est une fille.

Mother Une fille? Oh, shit! I name the child Eurydice Colette Clytemnestra Dido Bathsheba Rabelais Patricia Cocteau Stone. Now, take it away ... Bring me another lover.

scene thirteen Interior Edina's sitting-room. Day two. Later.

Patsy (*Dramatically.*) I could have been clever!

Saffron Could you?

Patsy Yes. I could have gone to university ... and all those years wasted ... and there you are rubbing it in. I resent you.

Edina No, you don't.

Patsy Yes, I do. (*To Saffron.*) I hate you. Just when my life hit a good patch, along you came, you miserable piece of flesh. You should have ended up in the dustbin – the incinerator was too good for you. You know, when I heard Ed was pregnant, I told her to abort. Abort! Abort! Abort! I said, chuck it down the pan, bring me ...

Saffron A knitting needle?

Patsy A knitting needle! Err! Oh . . . err!

Saffron slaps Patsy hard. Patsy tries to hit back. A fight ensues. Edina tries to break it up. She eventually manages to pull them apart. There is a tense silence. Eventually they settle down.

Edina Still, the more you quarrel the less you hate, that's what Sag Aloo says . . .

Saffron Don't take her side.

Edina I'm not on her side . . . (*Edina shakes her head and then nods to Patsy.*)

scene fourteen Interior. Edina's sitting-room. Day two. Later.

Edina, Patsy and Saffy are sitting in tense silence. The conversation then continues.

Patsy (*To Saffron.*) When you were three years old we tied you to the central reservation of the motorway.

Edina Shut up! (*To Saffron.*) Just one of Patsy's funny little jokes, darling. Anyway, you were like a homing pigeon. You were back within the week, sweetie.

Saffron What was my birth like?

Edina Your birth!

Patsy Ho-ho-ho!

Edina (*Glares at Patsy.*) Shut up, shut up! (*To Saffron.*) Beautiful, darling. It was gorgeous. It was lovely. I knew it was the best moment of my life, darling. It was like that . . . What's that, what's that lovely film? *Bambi*! It was like *Bambi*. In a little forest glade, darling. We were like those little . . . dogs, darling. What were they?

Saffron Deer.

Edina Deer! We were like those little deer, darling. It was lovely – so beautiful, sweetie.

scene fifteen Late 70s hospital. Flashback
Saffron's birth.

*Edina is in labour. It is a Jane Seymour fantasy birth. Justin is with her.
Patsy is sitting next to bed. Edina is very laid back, and the nurse is laying
roses on the bed.*

Edina (*Bravely enduring the labour pains.*) Ah! Oh! Oh! Oh!

Justin But, but you must have painkillers.

Edina (*Protesting.*) No, no, no. I don't need any painkillers.

Nurse You need drugs.

Edina Give the drugs to Patsy.

Nurse You're so brave.

Edina I know. I want this baby to be born on a carpet of roses.

Justin Roses.

Nurse Roses, roses, roses.

Edina I won't suffer any pain for this baby.

Scene fades.

scene sixteen Interior Edina's sitting-room.

Saffy is looking relaxed and happy. The conversation continues.

Edina It was lovely, darling. And from the moment you were born I
knew I wanted you, darling. I did. Mummy wanted you, sweetie.
Ohhh! (*They hug.*)

Patsy However, the day after . . .

Edina (*Rounds on Patsy and cuts her off in a way she has never done before.*)
Shut up!

*Patsy is shocked. Saffron is pleased. The door opens. It is like a vacuum being
pierced. Mother walks in.*

Mother Oh, it's rather stuffy in here, dear. Saffy, are you all right?
Why are you so close to your mother like that?

Edina We're just bonding. It's nothing you'd know about.

Patsy You coming to this party, Ed?

Edina Yes. (*To Saffron.*) See you then, darling.

Patsy and Edina exit.

Mother What's she been saying to you, dear?

Saffron Well, she's just been telling me about my birth, Gran.

Mother Oh, you know you mustn't believe a word your mother says, dear. Never mind – Gran's here now.

Edina (*Coming back in.*) Something in a blue kagoul is hovering outside.

Credits.

scene seventeen Return to flashback. Saffron's birth.

Edina is sitting on hospital bed holding baby Saffron. Patsy, dressed in black leather suit, is smoking and looking very bored.

Patsy Oh, look, are you coming to this party or what?

Edina I'm just waiting for the lady from the adoption agency to turn up. Just run along the corridor and see if you can see her, will you. I might just leave it with a note. (*To baby Saffron.*) Oh stop . . . Oh, what d'yer keep looking at me for? *What?*!

BULOUS